COUNTRIES OF THE WORLD

AFGHANISTAN

ABDO
Publishing Company

AFGHANISTAN

by Erika Wittekind

Content Consultant
Austin Long
Assistant Professor
School of International and Public Affairs, Columbia University

CREDITS

Published by ABDO Publishing Company, PO Box 398166, Minneapolis, MN 55439. Copyright © 2013 by Abdo Consulting Group, Inc. International copyrights reserved in all countries. No part of this book may be reproduced in any form without written permission from the publisher. The Essential Library™ is a trademark and logo of ABDO Publishing Company.

Printed in the United States of America,
North Mankato, Minnesota
112012
012013

 THIS BOOK CONTAINS AT LEAST 10% RECYCLED MATERIALS.

Editor: Rebecca Felix
Series Designer: Emily Love

About the Author: Erika Wittekind is a freelance writer and editor living in Wisconsin who has written more than half a dozen nonfiction books for children and young adults. She has a bachelor's degree in journalism and political science from Bradley University.

Cataloging-in-Publication Data

Wittekind, Erika.
 Afghanistan / Erika Wittekind.
   p. cm. -- (Countries of the world)
Includes bibliographical references and index.
ISBN 978-1-61783-625-1
1. Afghanistan--Juvenile literature.   I. Title.
958.1--dc22

2012946070

Cover: An Afghan woman walks past the remnants of the Buddhas of Bamiyan sculptures in the Bamiyan Mountains.

TABLE OF CONTENTS

CHAPTER 1
A VISIT TO AFGHANISTAN

As your flight makes its way to the Kabul International Airport in Afghanistan, you become increasingly nervous about what you will find in a country so often associated with conflict and war. You look out your window at the rugged landscape of the Hindu Kush Mountains and then finally the outlines of the dusty, sprawling city in their shadow.

On the ground in Kabul, Afghanistan's capital, the evidence of decades of war and unrest is everywhere. The city is an estimated 3,500 years old, but many of its oldest structures have been destroyed during various conflicts in the past 30 years. The remnants of ancient architecture now coexist with newer buildings that are a product of the country's slow reconstruction. Armored vehicles carry important or wealthy passengers. Security forces walk the streets to maintain order, and the nicer hotels, restaurants, and important buildings are surrounded by high gates and protected by armed guards.

The Hindu Kush Mountains tower behind Kabul, Afghanistan's capital.

The country wasn't always so forbidding. Until the 1970s, Afghanistan was a popular stop for travelers, drawing tens of thousands of visitors each year to its cultural and archaeological sites, exotic markets, and beautiful mountain landscapes. But the next few decades brought devastation to the natural surroundings and the people of Afghanistan. Conflict journalist Dexter Filkins spoke of his time in Afghanistan in 1998, when an oppressive group known as the Taliban had emerged. The Taliban was a fundamentalist political and religious group that ruled large parts of Afghanistan during the late 1990s. "It was a very strange time. The Taliban were so weird; it was like they were from another century, another galaxy. In those days I was just mystified by Afghanistan—what it was, where it was going," he said. "Any Westerner who was there—reporters or aid workers . . . felt exactly the same way. . . . We could tell things there were going bad, that they were headed toward some terrible end."[1] By 2012, with the exception

THE KHYBER PASS IN THE HINDU KUSH MOUNTAINS

One of the most well-known mountain passes in the world, the Khyber Pass was a popular way to enter Afghanistan before conflicts made passage difficult. The road weaves through the Hindu Kush Mountains and links Peshawar, Pakistan, to Torkham, Afghanistan, and on to Kabul. Historically, the Khyber Pass was an entrance point for invaders and traders to the country, including Persians, Greeks, Mughals, Afghans, and the British. The pass remains a major trade route from Pakistan into Afghanistan.

of aid workers, civilians working with the military, and a few experienced or adventurous travelers, war kept almost all visitors away from Afghanistan. But those who do venture to the capital find a lot to see beyond the dust and the rubble. "People love Kabul," one local tour guide told a *New York Times* reporter. "They've heard nothing positive about the place—that it was destroyed, that it's dangerous. Then they get here and get a big surprise—they see a bustling bazaar city, full of life."[2]

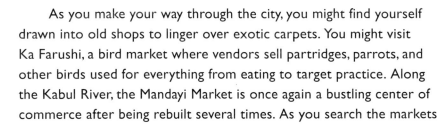

TRAVEL ADVISORIES

A weak central government, the remnants of war, and continued unrest have made Afghanistan a treacherous place to travel. As of 2012, the US State Department warned against all travel to Afghanistan, citing the hazards of ongoing military operations, bandits, land mines and other explosives, and the threat of violence between political and tribal rivals. In some cases, travelers and aid workers have been kidnapped and killed. In 2011, this included two German aid workers who were hiking in the mountains and an American civilian working at a Kabul power plant. Also that year, ten foreigners working for the United Nations (UN) Refugee Agency died in a bombing attack.

As you make your way through the city, you might find yourself drawn into old shops to linger over exotic carpets. You might visit Ka Farushi, a bird market where vendors sell partridges, parrots, and other birds used for everything from eating to target practice. Along the Kabul River, the Mandayi Market is once again a bustling center of commerce after being rebuilt several times. As you search the markets

for one of the country's world-famous carpets to take home, you might notice a group of boys flying kites, a favorite activity of Afghan youths. When you are done shopping, you find refreshment in one of Kabul's many teahouses. While sipping a cup of sweetened chai, you listen to the sounds of city traffic and the swirl of different languages being spoken around you, including Pashto and Dari.

The next day, you set out to see some of Kabul's more historic landmarks. High on your list is the recently restored Gardens of Babur in central Kabul, considered one of the city's most beautiful places. The gardens surround the tomb of Babur,

"Shafts of sunlight penetrated serpentine alleys lined by canvas-covered wooden stalls; the harsh light illuminated the bearded faces of Pashtun merchants and their bountiful wares: nuts, spices, dried fruits, tea, slabs of raw meat, live turkeys, blankets, beads of lapis lazuli. Sparks flew from the spinning wheels of knife sharpeners and strips of beef sizzled in huge pans of sesame oil. Adolescent boys careened through the passages pushing wheelbarrows, sending shoppers scurrying for safety; two butchers led a bleating black sheep to a rear courtyard for slaughter."[3]

—*Journalist Joshua Hammer describing the scene at the Mandayi Market*

Afghans sit among bright fabrics and other wares at an open-air bazaar in Kabul.

Visitors to Kabul's National Museum weave
past ancient wooden carvings that survived the
Taliban demolition of artifacts.

an emperor who ruled during the sixteenth century. The tomb was
designed by the same architect who created India's famous Taj Mahal.

In western Kabul, the Kabul Museum will give you a sense
of Afghanistan's long history, including the country's attempts to
pick up the pieces after its troubled recent past. The museum, also
called the National Museum of Afghanistan, once housed one of the

greatest collections of artifacts in Asia, with 100,000 pieces collected throughout 2,000 years of Afghan history. All but a few thousand artifacts were looted during periods of civil war following the Soviet occupation of the 1980s or later destroyed by the Taliban. But the museum was rebuilt in 2004 with an impressive display of salvaged and restored artwork. Wood carvings of eighteenth- and nineteenth-century deities and monarchs that had been demolished with axes and sledgehammers during Taliban rule were carefully pieced back together. Meanwhile, the stain of the country's violent recent history is purposefully on display at the Omar Museum, which displays land mines, tanks, and weaponry from the Soviet Union's invasion.

RECOVERY FROM WAR

Everywhere you go in Afghanistan, you will see the signs of a country trying to recover and move on from war. The country has been ravaged by conflict for more than three decades, beginning with the Soviet Union's invasion in 1979. Since then, the Afghan people have suffered periods of occupation, civil war, and the oppressive rule of the Taliban. But the course of Afghan history changed after September 11, 2001, when terrorists from the Islamist militant group al-Qaeda, based in Afghanistan, took control of four commercial airplanes in the United States. Two of those planes crashed into the twin towers of the World Trade Center in New York City, one hit the

Afghanistan means "Land of Afghans."

NORTH

1. KABUL
2. KAPISA
3. LAGHMAN
4. PANJSHIR

CHINA

UZBEKISTAN

⊛ Dushanbe

TAJIKISTAN

TURKMENISTAN

Amu Darya

Panj

Feyzabad
⊙

Langar
•

JOWZJAN
Sheberghan ⊙ Mazar-e Sharif
⊙

KONDOZ
Kondoz ⊙

BADAKHSHAN

BALKH
Sar-e Pol ⊙

Taloqan ⊙
TAKHAR

FARYAB
Meymaneh •

SAMANGAN
Samangan ⊙ • Baghlan
Pol-e Khomri ⊙

Bazarak •

SAR-E POL

BAGHLAN
Gulbahar •

4
Parun ⊙

BADGHIS

Jabal os Saraj • Mahmud-e Raqi ⊙

NURESTAN

Qal'eh-ye Now ⊙

35°

Bamiyan •

Charikar ⊙
PARWAN 1

2

3
KONAR
Asadabad ⊙

35°

Herat •
⊙

Chaghcharan ⊙
BAMIYAN

VARDAK
Meydan Shahr •

Kabul
⊛ • Bagram

Mehtar-Lam ⊙

INDIA

HERAT

GHOWR

Nili ⊙

LOWGAR

Jalalabad ⊙

Kabul

NANGARHAR
Torkham •

DAYKONDI

Pol-e 'Alam ⊙
Gardiz ⊙

Islamabad ⊛

FARAH

Ghazni ⊙
GHAZNI

PAKTIA KHOWST
Khowst •

ORUZGAN
Tarin Kowt ⊙

Sharan ⊙

Farah •
⊙

ZABOL

PAKTIKA

PAKISTAN

Lake
Saberi

Qalat ⊙

IRAN

Kandahar ⊙

Zaranj ⊙
NIMRUZ

Lashkar Gah ⊙
HELMAND

KANDAHAR

Helmand

30°

65°

70°

International boundary
Regional boundary
⊛ National capital
⊙ Regional capital
• City or village

0 _____ 100 Miles
0 _____ 100 Kilometers

Political Boundaries of Afghanistan

Pentagon in Washington DC, and a fourth was diverted into a field. When the Taliban regime refused to hand over al-Qaeda's leader, Osama bin Laden, the United States and its allies launched Operation Enduring Freedom. Within three months, those forces had toppled the Taliban regime in Afghanistan and driven the Taliban and al-Qaeda leaders to flee into Pakistan. Afghanistan held its first-ever democratic election in October 2004, and more than 80 percent of registered voters turned out at the polls.[4]

The road to peace has proved difficult, however. After a few years of relative calm, in 2006 Taliban insurgents began launching larger and more deadly attacks, including suicide bombings and improvised explosive devices (IEDs). As of 2012, the Taliban insurgency continued, and the young Afghan government struggled to maintain security. The new government, besieged by corruption, has been too weak to enforce laws in all sections of the country. Years of war, severe drought, and a series of oppressive regimes have brought widespread economic hardships, poverty, and illiteracy. Some Afghans fled the country, and many rural residents moved to urban areas in search of safety or work.

There are points of light on the horizon from this political shift, however. Many restrictions on freedom imposed under the oppressive Taliban have been lifted. Schools that were formerly only for boys have been reopened to girls as well as boys. Women have been allowed to seek employment outside the home again, which was forbidden under Taliban rule. Medical care has been established. Many Afghans are focused on getting on with their lives and finding ways to survive.

Afghans are diverse individuals, but their shared history unites them in their hope for peace.

As journalist Filkins explained in 2011 when asked what the Afghan people are looking for in general: "It's hard to generalize about the Afghans. They are diverse. But my experience of the war is this: You've got NATO [the North Atlantic Treaty Organization] over here, and the Taliban over there, and the vast majority of Afghans are caught in the middle. They just want peace. . . . Remember, they have not had a day of peace in that country for 32 years."[5] Known for their fierce independence, Afghans are eager to once again regain full control of their country and finally move on to a more peaceful existence.

SNAPSHOT

Official Name: Islamic Republic of Afghanistan

Capital city: Kabul

Form of government: Islamic republic

Title of leader: president

Currency: afghani

Population (July 2012 est.): 30,419,928
World rank: 40

Size: 251,827 square miles (652,230 sq km)
World rank: 41

Languages: Dari, Pashto

Official religion: Islam

Per capita GDP (2011, US dollars): $1,000
World rank: 213

CHAPTER 2

GEOGRAPHY: MOUNTAINS AND DESERT

Decades ago, Afghanistan was known more for its breathtaking views, historic sites, and opportunities for adventure than for its political unrest. Several hours north of Kabul, the Panjshir Valley is known as one of Afghanistan's most beautiful places. *Panjshir*, which means "five lions" in Dari, is also the name of the rushing Panjshir River, along which travelers enter through a narrow gorge that widens into a picturesque valley dotted with colorful crops and orchards—as well as destroyed Soviet armored vehicles, a reminder that this valley was the scene of some of the most intense conflict during the 1980s. The road through the valley leads north to both the Khawak Pass,

The city of Kabul has existed for approximately 3,500 years.

The Panjshir Valley is divided into five regions, and the Panjshir River runs through them all.

PANJSHIR VALLEY

Panjshir Valley, or Valley of the Five Lions, is named for the five brothers who dammed the river during the tenth century. The area is also known for its resistance to Soviet invaders during the 1980s. The tomb of Ahmad Shah Massoud, a military leader known for courageously fighting against the Soviets, is located in the valley.

a gateway through the Hindu Kush Mountains to the northern plains, and the Anjoman Pass, a route once used by the armies of Alexander the Great. As with many routes through Afghanistan, these rugged corridors are lined with both scenery and history.

The westernmost extension of the Himalayas, the Hindu Kush Mountains etch a jagged path through much of the country with towering peaks and dramatic valleys. *Hindu Kush* means "Hindu killer" in Dari, a testament to the danger of crossing these mountains. The high passes have been traversed by travelers, traders, and invaders alike over the centuries. While Afghanistan is best known for its mountain landscapes, the far north holds fertile farmland and the southwest contains dry, windy desert.

Located in southeast Asia, Afghanistan is entirely landlocked. It shares borders with Iran to the west; Pakistan to the south and east; and Turkmenistan, Uzbekistan, and Tajikistan in the north. In the far northeast corner of the country, it also shares a short border with China. These boundaries were established in the nineteenth century.

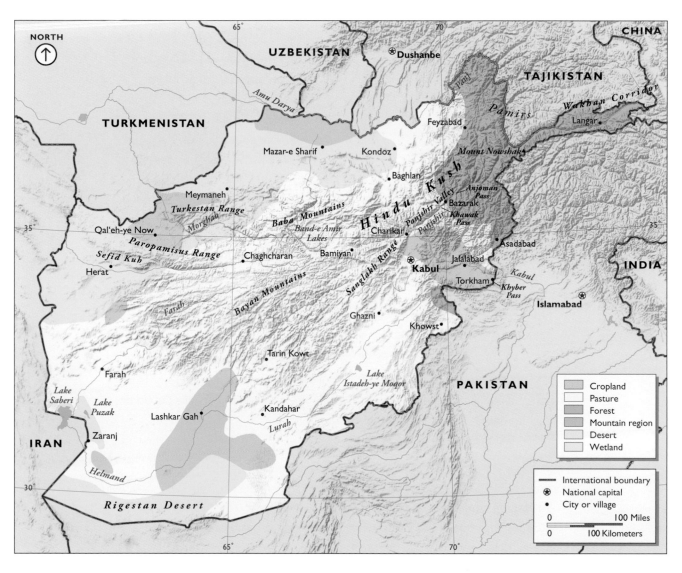

NORTH ↑

CHINA

UZBEKISTAN

⊛ Dushanbe

TAJIKISTAN

Amu Darya

TURKMENISTAN

Pamirs

Wakhan Corridor

Feyzabad

Langar

Mazar-e Sharif

Kondoz

Mount Nowshak

Baghlan

Hindu Kush

Meymaneh

Turkestan Range

Anjoman Pass

Baba Mountains

Bazarak

Panjshir Valley

Morghab

Band-e Amir Lakes

Khawak Pass

Qal'eh-ye Now

Paropamisus Range

Charikar

Panjshir

Sefid Kuh

Chaghcharan

Bamiyan

Sanglakh Range

Asadabad

Herat

⊛ Kabul

Jalalabad

INDIA

Bayan Mountains

Kabul

Farah

Ghazni

Torkham

Khyber Pass

Khowst

Islamabad ⊛

Tarin Kowt

Lake Istadeh-ye Moqor

PAKISTAN

Farah

Cropland

Lake Saberi

Lake Puzak

Pasture

Forest

Lashkar Gah

Lurah

Mountain region

Zaranj

Desert

Wetland

Helmand

International boundary

⊛ National capital

• City or village

Rigestan Desert

0   100 Miles

0   100 Kilometers

Geography of Afghanistan

HINDU KUSH FAULT LINES

Two major faults lines lie under the Hindu Kush Mountains in Afghanistan: the Chaman Fault and the Hari Rod Fault. Activity along these fault lines causes approximately 5,000 earthquakes every year.[1] Several of these have been extremely deadly. The resulting landslides in the mountainous country often add to the earthquake death toll. The cities of Jabal os Saraj and Gulbahar were destroyed by earthquakes in 1874. Approximately 2,000 people died in an earthquake in Lowgar Province in 1956. Earthquakes in Takhar and Badakhshan Provinces killed 4,000 people in 1998.[2]

With 251,827 square miles (652,230 sq km), Afghanistan is slightly smaller than the state of Texas. The country is divided into 34 provinces. The capital, Kabul, also Afghanistan's largest city, is located along the Kabul River, just south of the Hindu Kush Mountains. The second-largest city is Kandahar, which was the first capital of modern Afghanistan and is now the commercial center of the country's southern regions. Mazar-e Sharif is the urban center of northern Afghanistan, and Herat is a major trade and agricultural center in the west. Other major cities include Baghlan, Jalalabad, Kondoz, and Charikar.

GEOGRAPHICAL REGIONS

Stretching roughly from the southwest to northeast, Afghanistan's mountain ranges divide the country into three geographic regions: the central highlands, the northern plains, and the southwestern plateau. The central highlands consist of the main part of the Hindu

The Hindu Kush mountain range covers much of Afghanistan. Approximately half the country is at an elevation higher than 6,600 feet (2,000 m).

Kush Mountain range. The country's highest peak, Mount Nowshak, rises 24,557 feet (7,485 m) above sea level. One hundred miles (161 km) north of Kabul, the Hindu Kush split into a series of mountain ranges, including the Baba, the Bayan, and the Sefid Kuh. The country's major rivers all originate in the Hindu Kush Mountains of the central highlands. The Kabul River flows from the Sanglakh Range 45 miles (72 km) west of the capital, east into Pakistan. Also originating west of Kabul, in the Baba Mountains, the Helmand River flows southwest toward Iran.

North of the central highlands sit the northern plains. Approximately 40,000 square miles (103,000 sq km) of fertile plains and hills stretch from Iran to almost the border with Tajikistan. The Amu Darya, one of the longest rivers in central Asia, separates this region of Afghanistan from its northern neighbors Tajikistan, Uzbekistan, and Turkmenistan. The Amu Darya is also at the country's lowest elevation: 846 feet (258 m) above sea level. The access to water and the relatively low elevation, at an average of 2,000 feet (600 m) above sea level, make this a heavily farmed and densely populated area of the country.

South of the central highlands is the land known as the southwestern plateau. It consists of approximately 50,000 square miles (130,000 sq km) of arid and semiarid climates, with an average elevation of 3,000 feet (900 m) above sea level. In contrast to the northern plains, the soil in these areas is not very fertile away from the few major rivers, making farming difficult in much of the region.

LAKES

Landlocked Afghanistan has few significant lakes. There is Lake Saberi in the southwest and Lake Istadeh-ye Moqor in the southeast. The Band-e Amir ("Commander's Dam") Lakes in the Baba Mountains are well-known for their beautiful shades of blue—ranging from turquoise to a deep royal blue—created by the bedrock underneath.

CLIMATE

When it comes to climate, Afghanistan is a country of extremes. Winters are very cold and summers are very warm throughout most of the country, except for very high in the mountains,

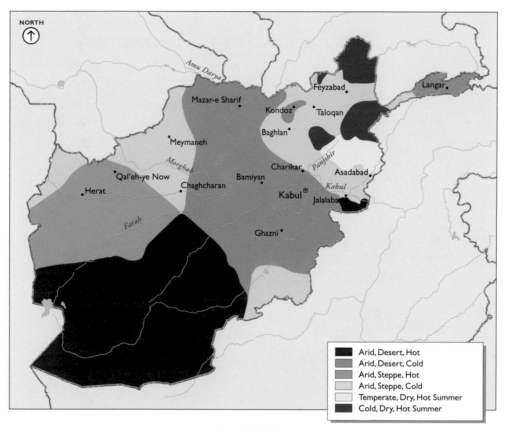

NORTH ↑

Amu Darya

Mazar-e Sharif

Feyzabad

Langar

Kondoz   Taloqan

Baghlan

Meymaneh

Morghab

Panjshir

Charikar

Asadabad

Qal'eh-ye Now

Bamiyan   *Kabul*

Herat   Chaghcharan   Kabul ⊛

Jalalabad

Farah

Ghazni

▮	Arid, Desert, Hot
▮	Arid, Desert, Cold
▮	Arid, Steppe, Hot
▮	Arid, Steppe, Cold
▮	Temperate, Dry, Hot Summer
▮	Cold, Dry, Hot Summer

Climate of Afghanistan

where it can be cold year-round. The high elevations of the central highlands create temperatures below freezing and snowfall in the winter. However, in some areas, such as Jalalabad, the heat is often extreme, reaching as high as 120 degrees Fahrenheit (49°C).[3] Most precipitation

AVERAGE TEMPERATURE AND PRECIPITATION

Region (City)	Average January Temperature Minimum/Maximum	Average July Temperature Minimum/Maximum	Average Precipitation January/July
Central Highlands (Kabul)	23/36°F (−5/2°C)	67/88°F (19/31°C)	1.3/0.2 inches (3.3/0.5 cm)
Northern Plains (Mazar-e Sharif)	29/50°F (−2/10°C)	78/102°F (26/39°C)	1.0/0.1 inches (2.5/.3 cm)
Southwestern Plateau (Farah)	33/61°F (1/16°C)	76/108°F (24/42°C)	0.5/0.0 inches (1.27/0.0 cm)[6]

occurs during the winter and spring months, with almost no rain falling from June to October.[4]

The arid and semiarid southwestern plateau experiences hot, dry, windy summers. Periods of drought and highs over 95 degrees Fahrenheit (35°C) are typical in the summer.[5] Winters are mostly dry and mild on the southwestern plateau, with occasional days of severe cold. The northern plains have similarly mild winters and hot summers, but

Afghan boys ride through a field in Kabul that flooded after a short spell of rain.

DESERT IRRIGATION

Because water is difficult to come by in the dry southern plateau region, Afghans built a system of underground canals called *karezes* to irrigate the land. This system was extensive in the eleventh and twelfth centuries. However, a Mongol invasion led by Genghis Khan in the thirteenth century destroyed much of this early irrigation system. The system has been partially rebuilt in some areas.

with more precipitation in the winter and spring. The only area of the country to receive much summer rain is the southeast corner bordering Pakistan, where the Indian monsoon season brings rain and humidity from July to September.

Sandy desert and arid steppe regions dominate the southwest region of Afghanistan and a small strip along the northern border.

CHAPTER 3

ANIMALS AND NATURE: RETURNING DIVERSITY

Perhaps the most recognized of Afghanistan's diverse animals is the Marco Polo sheep. They are named for explorer Marco Polo, the first person to describe them in Western writings. A typical Marco Polo sheep stands more than three feet (1 m) high, with spiral horns that extend approximately 60 inches (152 cm). Formally named *Ovis ammon*, Marco Polo sheep were plentiful in the wild when Polo first wrote about them. They are not as numerous now. The International Union for Conservation of Nature (IUCN) lists the Marco Polo sheep as near threatened. This means they are in danger of becoming vulnerable or endangered if populations continue to decrease. This species has been listed as protected in Afghanistan since 2009, but poaching continues with little enforcement. Marco Polo sheep can still be found in the Pamir

Marco Polo sheep typically live in herds with a few dozen others that are both female and male.

Mountains of the Wakhan Corridor. Afghanistan is home to many other species of sheep and goats as well, including urial sheep, Siberian ibex, and markhor, a type of goat with spiral-shaped horns. These species used to be much more common throughout the Hindu Kush but are now mostly found in the provinces bordering Pakistan.

Snow leopards, another noteworthy but declining native Afghan species, have also been on the nation's protected list since 2009. Snow leopards' large paws, thick fur, and long tail make them well suited for living in the mountains. The IUCN lists them as endangered, with an estimated 100 to 200 remaining high in the mountains of northeastern Afghanistan.[1] The population has declined due to habitat damage, poaching, and the killing of leopards thought to have preyed on livestock.

The only primate native to Afghanistan is the rhesus monkey, which lives in the forests of Nurestan.

Common leopards, however, continue to roam the central highlands and northern plains. Afghanistan is also home to other large mammals, including gray wolves, jackals, and small numbers of both brown and black bears. Tigers and cheetahs have disappeared from Afghanistan, but hyenas can still be found in the deserts of the south. More than 460 recorded species of birds are also found in Afghanistan.[2] Buzzards, mynahs, rock doves, and bulbuls are among the most common. Birds of prey, such as large vultures, live in the mountains.

Snow leopards are smaller than other types of leopards.

ENDANGERED SPECIES IN AFGHANISTAN

According to the International Union for Conservation of Nature (IUCN), Afghanistan is home to the following numbers of species that are categorized by the organization as Critically Endangered, Endangered, or Vulnerable:

Mammals	11
Birds	14
Reptiles	1
Amphibians	1
Fishes	5
Mollusks	0
Other Invertebrates	1
Plants	3
Total	36[4]

Plant life varies between regions. In the south, few plants can survive the hot, dry conditions of the desert, although even there some flowering plants bloom in the spring. At the other extreme, vegetation in the mountains north of Jalalabad benefits from an abundance of rainfall due to Indian monsoons. In between these areas, vegetation is mostly sparse, becoming denser in the east. Evergreen and deciduous forests used to cover 5 percent of the country's land area, but deforestation brought this down to just 2 percent as of 2009.[3] Pine forests remain in the high altitudes of the mountainous regions. Cedar, ash, oak, alder, walnut, and juniper trees grow at lower elevations, as well as shrubs, berries, and wildflowers. The northern plains, home to the most fertile soil, spring to life with wild tulips and other flowers in April and May.

CHALLENGES AND PROGRESS

War has taken a toll on Afghanistan's natural habitats and resources, both through direct destruction and through inattention to environmental issues during times of instability. Poaching of native species has gone unchecked by the government. Air pollution and water contamination have become problems in growing urban areas. Deforestation has occurred as forests are damaged by local farmers, refugees passing through, and smugglers who sell stolen timber in neighboring countries. The United Nations Environment Programme (UNEP) estimates that if Afghanistan's forests continue to be destroyed at the current rate, they will be gone within 30 years.[5]

PISTACHIO FORESTS

Pistachio forests used to cover much of the provinces of Badghis and Takhar in northern Afghanistan through the 1970s. For many Afghans, these trees were a source of food, firewood, and income. During the Soviet conflict of the 1980s, however, these forests were almost completely destroyed. Some trees were uprooted by the invaders, some were chopped down to stockpile firewood, and others were lost to forest fires that began as a result of the fighting.

Joe Walston, Asia program director of the Bronx Zoo in New York, which also works to protect animals in their natural habitats, explained how the conditions of war contribute to environmental problems: "Under times of stress or conflict, people are more willing to make short-term profits . . . because they feel insecure about the future."[6] However, the long-term preservation of resources is important to many Afghans who depend on wild game, firewood, and other natural resources to survive. According to a 2009 UNEP report, as much as 80 percent of the population depends on natural resources for their food and livelihood.[7]

Since 2002, the Afghan government has been cooperating with UNEP to create plans to undo the environmental damage of the past and put protections for the future into place. Afghanistan's National Environmental Protection Agency was created in

CHAMPIONS OF THE EARTH AWARD

In 2010, UNEP awarded Mustafa Zahir, director of Afghanistan's National Environmental Protection Agency and grandson of Afghanistan's last king, the Champions of the Earth Award. "Prince Zahir has transformed environmental policy and laid the foundation for sustainability in one of the most challenging countries on the planet at this moment in history," UNEP Executive Director Achim Steiner said.[8]

A young Afghan makes a painting for World Environment Day (June 5), which is supported by UNEP to encourage environmental preservation and protection.

NATIONAL PARKS

While several Afghan national parks, including Band-e Amir, were created during the 1970s, no legal protection was ever implemented to protect them. Because it was the first of these parks to have official protections put in place, Band-e Amir, established in 2009, is considered to be the country's first real national park. Other parks listed since the 1970s include the waterfowl sanctuaries of Ab-i-Estada at Ghazni and Kol-e Hashmat Khan in Kabul, a wildlife reserve at Ajar Valley, the Registan Desert Reserve in the south, and the Big Pamir wildlife reserve in the Wakhan Corridor.

2005. Since then it has been in charge of regulation and enforcement of environmental protections. However, its effectiveness has been limited due to the continued security issues in some parts of the country.

Although decades of conflicts have taken their toll on the wildlife of Afghanistan, the dedication of the country's first national park in 2009 demonstrated hope for recovery. Band-e Amir National Park, located in Bamiyan Province in eastern Afghanistan, was established on April 22, 2009. The area, which was a popular tourist destination during the 1950s, surrounds six mountain lakes. According to the Wildlife Conservation Society, the area has suffered from pollution, destruction of forests for firewood and farmland, overgrazing, and large game hunting.

The Bamiyan Province suffered from war and overuse of resources, but now the government works to protect it and to reintroduce tourists to the area's beauty.

Snow leopards, once native to the area, have all but disappeared.[9] Locals have even thrown hand grenades into the water as a way of fishing.

Designating this area as a national park prevents damaging development around the lakes and gives rangers more authority to enforce environmental laws. Beyond that, the new park represents a commitment to future stability and the protection of Afghanistan's natural habitats. "Seeing these crystal blue waters, set among the red cliffs and the travertine dams, shows the beauty in this land and the hope for the future," said US ambassador Karl Eikenberry at the park's dedication ceremony.[10] Mustafa Zahir, director of Afghanistan's National Environmental Protection Agency and grandson of the last king, hopes the landmark will become a "symbol of national unity" for his people.[11]

A bright blue lake is just one in a collection within Band-e Amir National Park.

CHAPTER 4

HISTORY: INVASIONS, UNREST, AND REVIVAL

Scientists estimate humans first settled in the area now known as Afghanistan as much as 100,000 years ago during the Paleolithic Era, or Old Stone Age. Although many archaeological artifacts were destroyed during wars and other conflicts, remnants do exist. Human bones discovered in the central highlands have been dated to approximately 30,000 years ago. These early hunter-gatherers lived in caves or built primitive dwellings on the plains. They used basic tools such as axes and spears. Evidence of early farming settlements from the Neolithic Era has also been found. One site near modern-day Kandahar dates to approximately 5000 BCE.

The oldest artifact in the Kabul Museum is estimated to be 3,500 years old.

Artifacts found near the northern city of Balkh have been estimated at 2,000 to 3,000 years old.

EARLY CONQUERORS

In premodern times, the area now known as Afghanistan was conquered by one foreign invader after another. "It had a positively magnetic quality for conquerors," wrote historian Thomas Barfield, "not because they coveted the wealth of Afghanistan, but rather because control of Afghan territory gave them access to more prosperous places like India or central Asia, or because it gave them control of regional trade routes."[1] These trade routes included the Silk Road, a notable route that made trade between Asia, the Middle East, and Europe possible between the third century BCE and the fifteenth century CE.

In approximately 2000 BCE, Aryan tribes—ethnic groups thought to speak Indo-European—migrated into the area of present-day Afghanistan, Iran, and India, bringing their language and culture to the area. In northern Afghanistan, they founded the city of Balkh, known as "mother of cities." Some modern Afghans are thought to have descended from these Aryan invaders.

Around the eighth century BCE, the Assyrians of Iran extended their rule into parts of Afghanistan. By approximately 600 BCE, a group of northern Iranian tribes called the Medes, who were closely related to the Persians, had moved into northern and western Afghanistan. Cyrus II, later known as Cyrus the Great, revolted against the king of the Medes and took over the empire in approximately 550 BCE. Led by Cyrus II, the Persians invaded Afghanistan through the southwestern desert. The Persians battled their way up to Bagram, near modern-day

Kabul, and then defeated Scythian tribes, nomadic Iranians who were living in the north by the Amu Darya. When Cyrus II was killed in battle, Darius I seized control of the Persian Empire, including Afghanistan.

By the middle of the fourth century BCE, the once wide-ranging Persian Empire was beginning to crumble. As this was happening, Alexander the Great ascended to the throne in Macedonia, an area inhabited by an ethnic group with unknown origins that controlled Greece and had adopted the Greek language. Alexander quickly executed anyone who posed a threat to his power and set his sights on expanding the boundaries of his realm. In 331 BCE, the Macedonian army battled its way through the Persian holdings, capturing city after city, leading him into modern-day Afghanistan. He established the city Alexandria of the Arians at the site of the modern-day city Herat, then continued trekking eastward through the Hindu Kush Mountains and past Kabul from 330 to 329 BCE. The Macedonians worked to secure the rest of the Persian Empire, including the area around Balkh in northern Afghanistan that was ruled by the Persian leader Oxyartes.

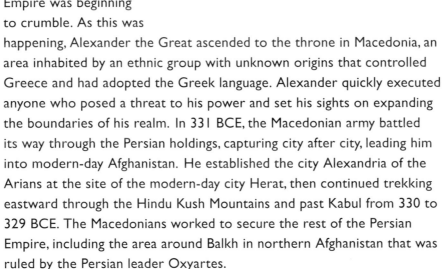

THE ARRIVAL OF THE GREEKS

Because some Greeks worked for the Persians as historians or military consultants, the first Greeks arrived in Afghanistan between 100 and 200 years before Alexander the Great's invasion. Much of what is known about the ancient Persian Empire comes from stories recorded by Greek historians at that time.

An ancient carving of Alexander the Great

Alexander died of illness in 323 BCE without an heir, leading to political disarray and the division of his kingdom. Despite founding many cities and spreading Greek culture, Alexander was unable to establish a lasting hold on his empire for his people.

The Greek Macedonians retained power in northern Afghanistan under one of Alexander's cavalry commanders, Seleucus I Nicator. Meanwhile, the Mauryan dynasty of India came to rule over southern Afghanistan, holding power there from 305 to 185 BCE. This was a peaceful time for southern Afghanistan. Indian emperor Asoka promoted the spread of Buddhism, which encourages respect for life and tolerance of other beliefs. In 185 BCE, a coup led by Indian leader Pusyamitra Sunga ended the Mauryan rule throughout southern Afghanistan. The new Indian government persecuted Buddhists and promoted Hinduism, which grew to become an important religion in Afghanistan. In the north, the province of Bactria seceded from the Seleucid Empire, becoming the Greco-Bactrian Kingdom. The Greco-Bactrians expanded their rule south to modern Kabul, while the Parthians of eastern Iran, who had been part of the Seleucid Empire but had declared their independence when Bactria and the Seleucid Empire split, moved into parts of southern Afghanistan.

In 135 BCE, five nomadic tribes who came to be known as the Kushans united to

THE BUDDHAS OF BAMIYAN

During their reign, the Kushans spread Buddhism throughout their kingdom and created one of Afghanistan's most famous landmarks. The world's tallest standing Buddha statues—measuring 175 feet (53 m) and 120 feet (37 m) tall, were carved into a cliff in the Bamiyan Mountains northwest of Kabul. The Taliban destroyed the two statues in 2001, but the remnants are still a popular destination for tourists.

overthrow the Bactrians. They ruled northern India, Afghanistan, and parts of central Asia for four centuries before their land broke apart into multiple kingdoms in the third century CE. The Persian Sassanids took over Afghanistan in 241 but had difficulty unifying it under their control. In 400, Afghanistan was invaded yet again—this time by the violent White Huns of central Asia. The Huns continued to battle with the Persians for several centuries until the Persians triumphed in the sixth century.

The Arabs invaded Afghanistan in 652 and brought the Islam religion with them. The region was under Islamic rule for more than 500 years, as part of the Ghaznavid Empire from 962 to 1151 and the Ghorid Empire from 1151 to 1205. These centuries were a prosperous age for Afghanistan during which lavish architecture, flourishing arts, and new irrigation systems facilitating agriculture were common. But this prosperity was not to last.

MONGOL RULE

From 1205 to 1219, Afghanistan was ruled by Shah Muhammad II as part of the Khwarezmid Empire of central Asia and Iran. In 1219, Mongolian ruler Genghis Khan sent a messenger to the shah in Afghanistan, proclaiming the Mongols now ruled over Afghanistan. The message was accompanied by gold, silver, and other riches, but a border commander confiscated the treasure and killed the convoy. When Genghis Khan found out about this, he sent another message ordering the shah to submit to his terms and to turn over the border commander for

The infamous Genghis Khan influenced many
Asian countries' histories through his invasions.

punishment. The shah refused, triggering a violent invasion. More
than 200,000 Mongol warriors swept into Afghanistan, carving a path of
death and destruction. Several cities were destroyed and the Mongols set

fire to the land and destroyed irrigation systems, crippling Afghanistan's agricultural economy for centuries to come.

After Genghis Khan's death in 1227, his kingdom broke apart. Some pieces of his lands were ruled by his descendants, while others fell back into the hands of Afghan peoples. Timur, a descendant of Genghis Khan, rose to power in 1370 and continued the Mongols' strategy of using destruction and massacres to unify the territories. By the end of the fourteenth century, his empire stretched from northern India to eastern Turkey, encompassing Afghanistan. Unlike their predecessors, the Timurid rulers rebuilt cities and encouraged the arts and learning.

Emperor Babur kept a journal and is thought to be the first ruler to do so.

At the start of the sixteenth century, Babur, a descendent of Genghis Khan and Timur, left his father's kingdom in the area of modern-day Uzbekistan. Babur raised an army and captured Kabul in 1504. Over the next few decades, he established the Mughal Empire, which included northern India and southeast Afghanistan, and made Kabul its capital. Although later emperors moved the center of the Mughal Empire to India, Babur wrote more favorably in his memoirs about his experiences in Afghanistan, and he became a celebrated figure in Afghan history.

While the Mughals ruled Kabul and eastern Afghanistan, the Safavids of Iran controlled Herat and much of northern and western Afghanistan during the sixteenth and seventeenth centuries. Kabul and Kandahar were both key passages into India, and the two empires fought over control of the two cities. The Safavids gained and lost control of Kandahar several times during this time period until winning it more decisively in 1622. In the mid-seventeenth century, the Uzbeks gained control of northern Afghanistan. By the end of the seventeenth century, the strength of the Safavids and Mughals in Afghanistan was waning, and local power shifted back to the native Afghan tribes.

THE FIRST AFGHAN STATE

The seeds of Afghan independence began to stir in Kandahar during the early eighteenth century, when Persian rulers tried to convert the local Sunni Muslim tribes to Shia Islam. The leader of the rebellion, Mirwais Khan Hotak, was imprisoned and sent to the court of Isfahan, located in modern Iran, where he observed that Persian power was in decline. After his release, he plotted to assassinate the governor of Kandahar. He then led the rebellion of the Pashtun tribes, who were followers of Sunni Islam, and defeated the weak Persian army to establish Kandahar's independence in 1708. After Mirwais's death in 1715, his family members fought for control and briefly expanded their realm beyond Kandahar.

Fighting within the group and a lack of unity made the Afghans vulnerable to a pushback from the Persians. Persian ruler Nadir Shah secured control of the country by 1738. When he was assassinated in 1747, his empire quickly began to disintegrate, and the Persians once again lost control of Afghanistan. A council of local tribal leaders

Nadir Shah survived a failed assassination attempt in 1741.

Afghans regard Ahmad Shah Durrani as Ahmad Shah Baba, or "father of Afghanistan."

in southern Afghanistan selected Ahmad Shah Durrani, who had been a commander of Nadir Shah's Afghan bodyguard, to rule. The Durrani Empire quickly expanded, eventually stretching from the Amu Darya to the Arabian Sea, and from Meshed, Iran, to Delhi, India. A native Pashtun of Afghanistan, Ahmad Shah strove to subdue and unify the land's numerous different cultures into one country.

After his death in 1772, his successors—including his son, Timur Shah Durrani, and his grandson, Zaman Shah Durrani—failed to continue Ahmad Shah's unifying success. The next 50 years were marked by numerous rebellions and civil wars in Afghanistan. During the reigns of Shah Shoja Durrani and Shah Mahmud Durrani in the early nineteenth century, Great Britain negotiated a treaty with Afghanistan to protect its holdings in India. Under the agreement, Afghanistan agreed to resist the military of any other country—particularly France or Russia—that might try to reach India through Afghanistan. However, by 1818 Afghanistan was not in a position to uphold such an agreement, as Mahmud Durrani was incapable of controlling all of Afghanistan. Local tribes ruled the rest of the country. Mahmud made another misstep when he blinded and executed one of his supporters, Fatteh Khan. The man's younger brother, Dost Mohammad Khan, had risen to a position of power in Kabul, and he retaliated by overthrowing Mahmud in 1826. Dost Mohammad was the first of what would become the Barakzai Dynasty, ruling in Kabul, Jalalabad, and Ghazni.

CONFLICT WITH BRITAIN

Not wanting to submit to foreign occupation, Dost Mohammad nullified the treaty with Britain and opened communications with Persia and Russia. Persia tried to take over Herat in 1837, and the British grew increasingly fearful of losing their power in the region. After a diplomatic mission to Kabul failed to convince Dost Mohammad to accede to British demands to control Afghan foreign policy, British governor-general Lord Auckland of India ordered an invasion of Afghanistan in 1839. This marked the beginning of the First Anglo-Afghan War, which was intended to restore the former British ally Shah Shoja to power. The British succeeded, and Dost Mohammed fled Kabul. Following their victory, most of the British soldiers returned to India. In 1840, Dost

A depiction of the First Anglo-Afghan War

Mohammad surrendered to the British and remained a prisoner for the next two years. Some Afghans, however, were resentful of the British and continued to resist the newly restored Shah Shoja. Rebellions continued throughout the country, and the British decided to leave in 1842. Only a handful of men survived the nearly continuous Afghan attacks during the British retreat from Kabul to Jalalabad. The British launched reprisal attacks, but then left Afghanistan and freed Dost Mohammad.

Dost Mohammad returned to power and spent two decades working to unify Afghanistan. In 1854, he negotiated the Treaty of Peshawar with the British, which recognized the country's sovereignty and the integrity of its territory. After his death, Dost Mohammad's son Shir 'Ali Khan assumed power. Under his rule, the country's relationship with Britain once again declined. In 1878, Shir 'Ali refused to meet with a British envoy to Kabul, setting off the Second Anglo-Afghan War. After Shir 'Ali died in 1879, his son Ya'qub Khan signed the Treaty of Gandamak, giving Britain extensive control over Afghanistan. This made the Afghan people furious, and they rebelled. The British army prevailed over the Afghan fighters, but Britain decided that the cost of maintaining forces in Afghanistan was too high. Wrote historian Meredith Runion:

> The British realized that controlling Afghanistan as a buffer
> state would require controlling the dissenting Afghan people, and
> even defeating them did not mean they had overpowered their
> strong-willed spirits.[2]

In 1881, the British departed after putting 'Abd al-Rahman Khan, a nephew of Shir 'Ali, in power. Called the "Iron Amir" due to his tough policies, 'Abd al-Rahman focused on establishing the power of the central government in Kabul during his 20-year reign, fighting many wars against Afghan rivals while leaving foreign policy in the hands of the British. Some historians consider him to be the founder of modern Afghanistan. The consequences of his reign are still felt in Afghanistan, most notably due to his agreement with the British marking the border with British India. This border remains the Afghan border with Pakistan even though neither the Afghans nor the Pakistanis formally ratified it. In addition, 'Abd al-Rahman relocated rebellious Pashtun tribesmen to the north, where their descendants still live today, and conquered the remote region of Kaffirstan, or "land of the unbelievers," forcibly converting the inhabitants of what is now the province of Nurestan, or the "land of light," to Islam.

When 'Abd al-Rahman died in 1901, his son Habibullah Khan took power. During his 18-year reign, Habibullah worked to modernize Afghanistan, implementing Western-style technology and education. Despite pressure to join the Central powers during World War I (1914–1918), Afghanistan remained neutral. Family members who had wanted Habibullah to join the war against Britain assassinated him in 1919.

Prince Amanullah Khan, an Afghanistan nationalist, then rose to power as king. Amanullah wanted to end Britain's occupation and control of Afghanistan's foreign policy. In May 1919, he launched an attack on British-controlled India that started the Third Anglo-Afghan War. The British responded with an aerial assault, the first in Afghanistan's history. The Treaty of Rawalpindi established Afghanistan's foreign policy independence from Britain on August 8, 1919. Amanullah created the country's first constitution and civil rights code in 1923 and spent the rest of his rule trying to enact reforms to modernize Afghanistan. These reforms included abolishing slavery, introducing Westernized styles of dress, establishing education for both men and women, and creating a standard currency. Opposition to some of these reforms by more traditional Afghans led to civil war that forced Amanullah's resignation in 1929.

A Tajik rebel of Persian descent seized power briefly in 1929, but he was overthrown by a cousin of Amanullah, Mohammad Nader Shah, within months. Nader Shah abolished many of his cousin's reforms and instituted a new, more conservative constitution in 1931. New restrictions on free speech were put in place, leading to the imprisonment or execution of many outspoken intellectuals. A teenage student unhappy with the rollbacks on civil rights shot and killed the king in 1933. The boy and members of his family were killed as punishment.

THE END OF THE MONARCHY

The last king of Afghanistan was also the longest serving. Mohammad Zahir Shah, son of Nader Shah, held power from 1933 to 1973. Only 19 years old when he became king, Zahir Shah relied heavily on advisers and allies to help him rule. Under Zahir Shah and his advisers, Afghanistan reached out to Germany for aid in improving its

Zahir Shah in 1963

infrastructure and military. In 1934, Afghanistan was admitted into the League of Nations and officially recognized by the United States. During World War II (1939–1945), Afghanistan once again asserted its neutrality. After the war, the country experienced a brief return to liberalism. Different political groups were tolerated, debate was allowed, and newspapers were published freely. Prime Minister Sardar Shah Mahmud, the king's uncle and one of those helping to keep the young ruler in power, ended this age of tolerance in 1951, much to the disappointment of the country's youth. He served as prime minister from 1946 to 1953.

Throughout the 1950s, Afghanistan's government remained repressive. The Soviet Union began sending economic aid to the country during this time. However, as Zahir Shah grew stronger and became better able to rule, some reforms for women were enacted. Women no longer had to wear a veil or stay out of sight in public as before. In 1964, a loya jirga, or "grand assembly," approved a new constitution establishing a constitutional monarchy with a bicameral legislature. It emphasized individual freedoms and secular law. Elections took place in 1965 and 1969. However, modernization led to instability, as Zahir Shah changed too much for some but too little for others. In 1973, Mohammed Daud Khan, the king's cousin and a former prime minister, took advantage of the situation and seized power in an almost bloodless coup while the king was out of the country. Daud Khan ended the monarchy, did away with the 1964 constitution, and established a republican government with himself as its first president.

THE SOVIET INVASION AND CIVIL WAR

Daud Khan tried to move Afghanistan away from socialism and dependency on the Communist Soviet Union. As that relationship worsened, he reached out to other countries for assistance. But Afghanistan's economic difficulties and political instability persisted. In 1978, a leftist coup overthrew the government and established the Democratic Republic of Afghanistan. The new Communist regime was headed by Nur Mohammad Taraki and the Marxist-based political party the People's Democratic Party of Afghanistan (PDPA).

Russia and Britain's battle over central Asia, which involved Afghanistan, was called the Great Game.

When the Afghan people rebelled against the new government, the PDPA officially requested assistance from the Soviet Union. At the same time, there was infighting within the PDPA, and Taraki was assassinated and replaced by Hafizullah Amin. The Soviets, frustrated by the infighting and concerned that Amin might betray them, intervened in December 1979 and occupied the country for nine years. Afghans who rebelled against Communist rule were called mujahideen. The mujahideen rebels were assisted by the United States, the United Kingdom, China, Pakistan, Iran, Saudi Arabia, Jordan, and Egypt. The organization that would eventually become al-Qaeda was also created during this period by Osama bin Laden, a Saudi Arabian of Yemeni descent, to support the mujahideen. As the civil war and occupation continued, as many as 6 million Afghan refugees fled into Pakistan and Iran.[3]

By the time Mikhail Gorbachev took power in the Soviet Union in 1985, the costly war in Afghanistan had become increasingly unpopular worldwide. Gorbachev blamed Afghanistan's puppet government for failure to rule effectively and began withdrawing Soviet troops in 1988. By the war's end, approximately 14,500 Soviet troops and hundreds of thousands of Afghans had been killed in the conflict.[4]

THE TALIBAN

Conflict in Afghanistan continued for three more years until the Communist government was overthrown in 1992. The mujahideen and warlords who had previously supported the Communist regime began fighting among themselves in a devastating civil war, with several warlords competing for control. Refugees returning to the country were greeted by poverty and lawlessness. Thousands of people continued to be killed, and major destruction occurred. In this chaos, the Taliban rose to power. The Taliban was comprised of Sunni Muslim religious students, primarily Pashtuns, who believed in strict adherence to Islamic law. They established the Islamic Emirate of Afghanistan in 1996 and had secured the vast majority of the country by 2000. Other groups—primarily Tajiks, Uzbeks, and Hazaras— continued fighting against the Taliban. These groups, mostly in the north of the country, would eventually be called the Northern Alliance.

THE ORIGINS OF THE TALIBAN

The most common story told about the origins of the Taliban is that a Muslim cleric named Muhammad Omar was disgusted by reports that the mujahideen were torturing young prisoners. He led a group of 50 students into a mujahideen camp to free two teenage girls who were being sexually assaulted and tortured there. The group then rescued a young boy who was a prisoner in another camp. With these successes, the movement gained support and began traveling around the countryside to defeat rebel groups.

The Taliban instituted strict Islamic policies. Men were not allowed to shave their beards, and women could not go out in public unless completely covered with an Afghan burqa. Those in violation were subject to strict penalties. One woman who showed her fingertips in

Osama bin Laden

public had them cut off. Wearing makeup or nail polish was punishable by being beaten or burned with acid.

In 1996, bin Laden and other members of al-Qaeda returned to Afghanistan. The Taliban and al-Qaeda had similar fundamentalist views but different goals. The Taliban was focused on ruling Afghanistan, while al-Qaeda had much grander goals of removing US influence from Islamic lands and overthrowing what it viewed as the corrupt government of Saudi Arabia.

Al-Qaeda was thought to be behind several terrorist attacks, including the bombings of US embassies in Tanzania and Kenya in 1998. The Taliban government refused to extradite members of al-Qaeda for those acts. On September 11, 2001, al-Qaeda attacked the World Trade Center in New York City and the Pentagon in Washington DC. When it became clear that the Taliban was unwilling to hand over bin Laden and other al-Qaeda members after the attacks, the United States responded by supporting the Northern Alliance against the Taliban, swiftly removing the group from power. The Taliban fled to Pakistan, where it regrouped and then began a guerilla war in Afghanistan. Meanwhile, a new democratic government was established. An interim government was appointed until elections took place in 2004, when Hamid Karzai was selected as president.

CHAPTER 5

PEOPLE: DIVERSITY AND INDEPENDENCE

Several millennia of invaders and settlers in Afghanistan resulted in a patchwork of peoples that remains today. The many cultures and beliefs found throughout the country have caused great difficulty when it comes to sustaining a unified nation. But while ethnic diversity has frequently caused tensions, many Afghans do share social customs and traditions, including a commitment to hospitality and a fierce independence.

Experts have questioned the accuracy of population information for Afghanistan because censuses are rarely completed and ethnic groups tend to inflate their membership numbers for political reasons. As of 2012, the US Central Intelligence Agency estimated 30.4 million people resided in Afghanistan, ranking fortieth among the world's

Although two ethnicities make up the majority of the Afghan population, a blend of ethnicities can be found in the nation.

countries.[1] The two main ethnic groups in Afghanistan are the Pashtuns, comprising approximately 42 percent of the population, and the Tajiks, which make up approximately 27 percent. Other peoples living in Afghanistan include the Hazara (9 percent), the Uzbek (9 percent), the Aimak (4 percent), the Turkmen (3 percent), the Baloch (2 percent), and small numbers of other ethnicities (4 percent).[2]

> As of 2011, only one Jew was known to live in Afghanistan.

Across all of these peoples, religion is one near-constant: almost 100 percent of Afghans are Muslim— that is, people who believe in the religion of Islam. However, Afghan Muslims are divided between the two major branches of Islam. Eighty percent of Afghans adhere to Sunni Islam and 19 percent are Shi'ites, meaning they believe in and practice Shia Islam practices.[3] Hindus and Sikhs make up most of the remaining 1 percent of the population, although many members of these groups left during wartime.[4]

Religion pervades almost every aspect of Afghan life, from daily interactions and customs to government and politics. "Afghanistan is an example of an older form of Islamic society in which religion is not an ideology but remains an all-encompassing way of life," wrote historian Barfield. "Its influence is ever present in people's everyday conversations, business transactions, dispute resolutions, and moral judgments. There is no relationship, whether political, economic, or social, that is not validated by religion."[5]

PASHTUNS

There is great diversity within Afghanistan's many ethnic groups, although most of them are Sunni Muslims.[6] The Pashtuns encompass approximately 60 smaller tribal groups.[7] The largest of these are the Durrani, located south of Kabul, and the Ghilzai, located east of Kabul. Other significant Pashtun tribes include the Shinwari, the Mohmand, the Safi, the Khugiani, the Mangal, the Jadran, the Tani, the Jaji, and the Wardak. The majority of Pashtuns live along the eastern border with Pakistan, as well as across the north and far south. Smaller numbers live scattered throughout the interior of the country as well. Large numbers of Pashtuns also live in neighboring Pakistan.

SUNNI AND SHIA ISLAM

Followers of Islam are called Muslims. Muslims worship the god Allah and believe Allah's will is contained in the sacred text of the Koran. The contents of the Koran were communicated through Allah's messenger, Muhammad. The two branches of Islam evolved out of a disagreement over whom Muhammad's rightful successor should have been. The Shi'ites believe his power should have gone to his closest male relative, Ali, while the Sunnis wanted a leader who was more politically powerful. The divide was further cemented when Hussein, a son of Ali, challenged Sunni leadership and was killed along with his family. In modern times, a small number of Sunni and Shia fundamentalists have supported terrorism. However, most religious leaders of both branches condemn such acts of violence.

Boys from Pashtun and Pashai tribes of eastern Afghanistan

Most Pashtuns define themselves through their common ancestry, the Pashto language, and their adherence to a set of customs called Pashtunwali. However, due to geographic differences, not all Afghans who identify themselves as Pashtuns speak Pashto or follow the same tribal customs. According to their own lore, the Pashtuns originally descended from Afghana, the grandson of King Saul of Israel. Some historians think the Pashtuns are actually descended from the Aryan tribes that invaded in approximately 2000 BCE, mixed with later invaders. Author Barfield believes the Pashtun trace their ancestry to a common ancestor known as Qais.[8]

Each tribe occupies a specific territory and is descended from a common ancestor. Tribes are subdivided into clans, subclans, and families. Most Pashtuns live in rural areas as either farmers or herdsman, but many also enlist in the military. The Pashtuns have been politically powerful since the eighteenth century, when a tribal council appointed Ahmad Shah Durrani as ruler. The Durrani Pashtuns were in power almost continuously from 1826 to 1978. In 1978, power shifted to the Ghilzai Pashtuns, who created the Democratic Republic of Afghanistan. The Taliban was also Pashtun.

PASHTUNWALI

The Pashtuns follow a moral and legal code called Pashtunwali. This detailed code governs all areas of tribal life. It emphasizes values that include honor, justice for insults or misdeeds, personal responsibility, hospitality to those in need, solidarity, and bravery. Some of these values are defended to the death. However, decades of war have weakened the power of Pashtunwali in many parts of Afghanistan.

TAJIKS AND OTHER ETHNIC GROUPS

Tajiks, Afghanistan's second-largest ethnic group, are primarily of Persian descent but also have Arab, Greek, and Turkic ancestry. Most are Hanafi Sunni Muslim, although a small number are Ismaili Shia. Unlike the Pashtuns, Tajiks are no longer divided into tribes. Some Tajiks identify themselves by the name of the region they live in. They live primarily in the Panjshir Valley north of Kabul and in the northern provinces as farmers or herders. However, there is also a large Tajik population in Kabul, where they work in business, government, or other jobs. The Tajiks have a long-standing political rivalry with the Pashtuns. The Tajiks resisted the Taliban takeover and held onto a small fraction of the country during Taliban rule as part of the Northern Alliance that assisted the United States in overthrowing the Taliban in 2001.

Tajikistan borders Afghanistan in the northeast and is the historic homeland of ethnic Tajiks.

Members of the Hazara ethnic group live primarily in the central mountainous area, an area known as Hazarajat, or "Land of the Hazara." The Hazaras are thought to have Mongol ancestry. Most Hazaras are Imami Shia, while smaller numbers are either Ismaili Shia or Sunni. Due to prejudice against Shi'ites, the Hazara have been excluded from political positions and have been persecuted at times. Starting in the nineteenth century, the Pashtuns in power attacked Hazara communities, killing the Hazaras or forcing them to vacate their lands. Some Hazara women

Hazara women taking a rest in Bamiyan

were enslaved until the abolition of slavery in the early twentieth century. More recently, the Taliban targeted the Hazaras for ethnic cleansing and committed crimes against them. Since the fall of the Taliban, however, the Hazaras have begun participating in political parties and government.

The Uzbeks live in the northwest and are thought to have descended from nomadic tribes. They are Sunni Muslim. Some are farmers or herders, while others work in cities in skilled trades or business. Another Sunni Turkic-speaking ethnic group is the Turkmen. Once nomadic and warlike, the Turkmen now work as farmers, herders, and skilled artisans.

LANGUAGE

The two official languages of Afghanistan are Dari and Pashto. Dari is a form of Persian similar to Farsi, which is spoken in Iran. It is closer to what was spoken during the Persian Empire than Farsi. Dari uses a version of the Arabic alphabet and includes some words that also exist in the Persian or Arabic languages. It is the primary language of the Tajiks and the Hazaras. Approximately half of the population speaks various dialects of Dari.[9] The Hazaras, for example, speak a dialect of Dari called Hazaragi. Even ethnic groups that do not primarily speak Dari often use it as a second language, and it is the language most often used for interethnic communication. Dari has traditionally been the language used in politics, business, and trade in Afghanistan,

Bilingualism is common in Afghanistan.

even while the Pashtuns were in power.

Pashto is the primary language of the Pashtun tribes and is spoken by 35 percent of the population.[10] The dialect spoken in the southwest is simply called Pashto, while the eastern dialect is called Pukhto. Pashto uses an expanded version of the Arabic alphabet and is more grammatically complicated than Dari.

Eleven percent of the population—especially the Uzbeks and Turkmen—speak Turkic languages. The Uzbeks speak a Turkic language called Uzbeki. Another 4 percent speak one of 30 other languages, particularly Balochi and Pashai.[11]

CHANGING DEMOGRAPHICS

Decades of war pushed some Afghans to leave their country and still others to abandon their rural homes and move to larger cities. Since 1979, an estimated 6 million Afghan refugees have fled to Iran

YOU SAY IT!

English	Dari	Pashto
Peace (informal greeting)	Salam (sah-LAHM)	Salam (sah-LAHM)
Peace be upon you (formal greeting)	Assalam alaikum (ahs-SAH-lah-moh ah-LAY-koom)	Assalam alaikum (ahs-SAH-lah-moh ah-LAY-koom)
How are you?	Haletan chetor hast? (HAHL-uh-ton chuh-TOR ahst)	Ta tsanga yei? (ta SAHN-guh yay)
Good-bye	Khoda hafez (HOH-dah hah-FEZ)	De kuday pe aman (dah kho-DAY pah ah-MAN)
Thank you	Tashakor (tahsh-uh-KOHR)	Manana (mah-NAH-nah)

or Pakistan, and several million more have relocated within the country.[12] By 2009, approximately 5 million refugees had returned to Afghanistan.[13] Due to continued security issues, many returning Afghans went to Kabul or other major cities in search of homes and work. As of 2010, approximately 23 percent of the population lived in urban areas, a number that was increasing at a rate of 4.7 percent annually.[14]

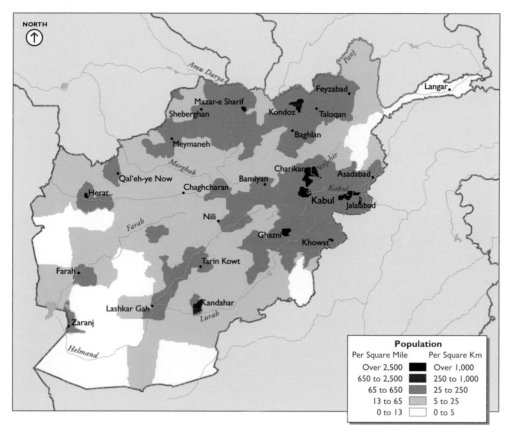

NORTH

Population

Per Square Mile		Per Square Km
Over 2,500	■	Over 1,000
650 to 2,500	■	250 to 1,000
65 to 650	■	25 to 250
13 to 65	■	5 to 25
0 to 13	□	0 to 5

Population Density of Afghanistan

Across all areas of the country, access to adequate medical care is a continual concern. Afghanistan's infant mortality rates (121.63 deaths per 1,000 live births) and maternal mortality rates (1,400 deaths per 100,000 births) are the twenty-first highest rates in the world. The overall death rate is eighth highest, with 14.59 deaths per 1,000 people per year. Life expectancy at birth is 49.72 years, ranking Afghanistan at 217 out of 221 ranked countries.[15]

Afghan newborns in a Kabul hospital. Although Afghanistan has a high birth rate, life expectancy is low.

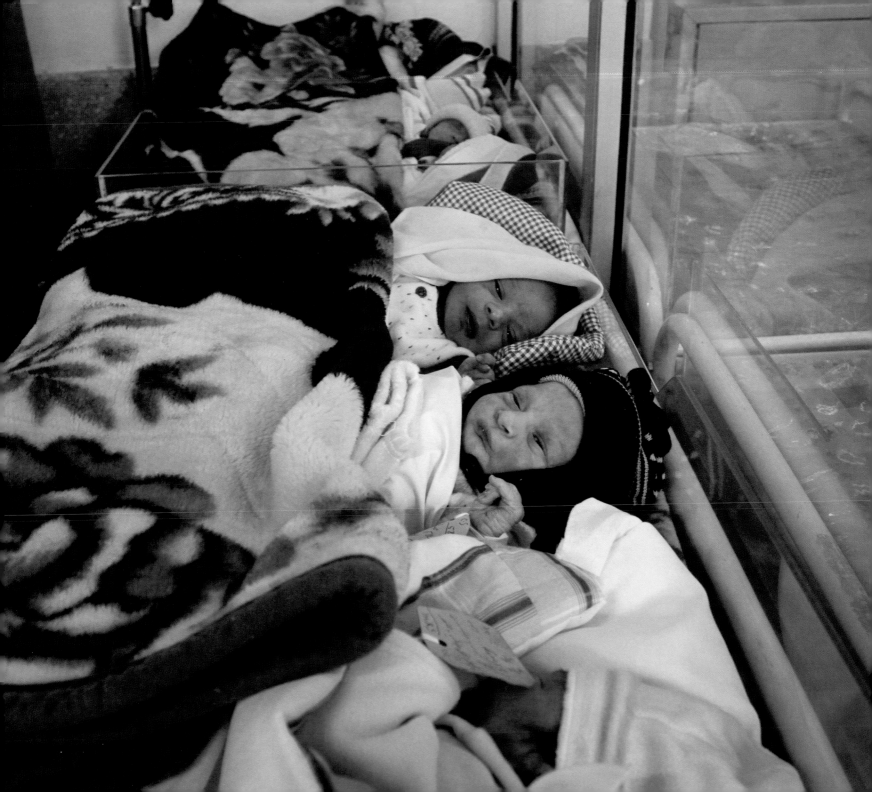

CHAPTER 6

CULTURE: THRIVING TRADITIONS

Afghanistan's most significant form of folk art is perhaps its world-renowned hand-knotted carpets. Turkmen in the northwest—primarily women working at home—traditionally produce these carpets. A network of weavers in the countryside may often work together on individual carpets, which can take up to nine months to finish. More than 1 million Afghans were employed in carpet production work as of 2007, according to the Afghanistan Carpet Exporters Guild.[1] Historically, the Turkmen were a nomadic people, and they wove carpets, tents, and other items out of wool because they were easily transportable. Nowadays, these carpets have both trade value and social meaning. Across Afghanistan, carpets are often included in a girl's wedding dowry. The number of carpets a family has is an indicator of its wealth or social standing. The carpets are usually colored in deep reds or ochres, and they often have a pattern of stylized flowers, animals, or trees. Another

Woven photograph-like depictions, rich colors, and intricate patterns are trademarks of Afghan carpets.

popular design is called *filpai*, or "elephant's foot." It is a pattern of medallions laid out in a shape that resembles an elephant's footprint.

Traditionally, Afghan carpets were known for the distinct geometric patterns and designs they displayed. Until the early 1980s, certain designs or patterns were often associated with specific tribes or areas. During the 1980s, carpet weavers defied tradition and started using war imagery, such as aircraft, weaponry, and maps. Later, carpets were made that depicted the 2001 attack on the World Trade Center. These particular carpets were made to be sold to Westerners to commemorate the day, but many Westerners criticized them as exploitative.

MUSIC AND DANCE

Classical Afghan music is heavily influenced by musicians who were brought to the royal court from India during the nineteenth century. The instruments used in such music are similar to those used in other countries in the region and include a short-necked lute called a *rabab*, a long-necked lute called a *dutar*, and Indian drums called tabla. The country's most famous classical musician was Ustad Mohammed Qasim Afghan, who was popular during the 1920s. He is sometimes called the father of Afghan music.

The country's folk music varies between ethnic groups. Rhythms created by drums tend to be prominent. The drums used in Afghan folk music include the *dohol*, which is barrel shaped, and the *zirbaghali*, which is shaped like a goblet. The *daff* has a flat frame and is the only instrument traditionally played by women. Other instruments are not forbidden, but it is frowned upon for women to play them. Weddings, holidays, and other celebrations are enriched with folk dancing called *atan* in which both genders participate.

Under the Taliban regime, all forms of music other than religious chanting were banned. Musicians' instruments were smashed, and cassette recordings were confiscated and destroyed. Several Afghan performers, including singer Farhad Darya, left the country to continue their careers. Darya found refuge in the United States. Some Afghan musicians have returned to their home country

HOLIDAYS

The most significant holidays celebrated in Afghanistan are the Muslim religious holidays. The monthlong holiday Ramadan features fasting in the daytime followed by evening celebration. Eid al-Fitr is a festival that lasts for one to three days following Ramadan, marking the end of the fast.

Eid al-Adha is a festival remembering the sacrifice of Ishmael, a story told in the Koran. Lambs or cows are sacrificed, and the meat is shared among family and friends. Muslims also celebrate Maulud-Sharif, the birth of the Prophet Muhammad.

In the twentieth century, Afghans also started celebrating several secular holidays, including Nawruz (New Year's Day) on March 21, the first day of spring; Jeshen (Independence Day) on August 19, which celebrates the anniversary of gaining independence from Great Britain in 1919 with the Treaty of Rawalpindi; and Labor Day on May 1.

or come out of hiding since the fall of the Taliban, despite continued violence. But since many performers of traditional Afghan music have aged or continued living abroad, some worry these traditions will be discarded in favor of more popular Western music.

POETRY

Living in a country in which their freedom has been heavily restricted, a portion of the literate women of Afghanistan express themselves by writing poetry. While women officially gained rights after the fall of the Taliban, these reforms have not been carried out in rural areas. Most young women still lack access to education, are forced to marry young, and are kept in seclusion. As of 2000, less than 13 percent of women were literate.[2] However, of that small percentage, many women write poetry in secret as a form of rebellion and as a way to express themselves. A popular type of folk poetry is the *landai*, which translates to "short, poisonous snake" in Pashto. These poems often include biting commentary on life in Afghanistan from a woman's perspective. Landais are two-line poems that are composed anonymously and then shared and repeated among Afghan women. "Landai belong to women," explained Safia Siddiqi, a well-known Pashtun poet. "In Afghanistan, poetry is the women's movement from the inside."[3] Landais deal with many subjects, including love, marriage, and grief, as well as social or political issues such

Farhad Darya in concert in Kabul

as Afghan independence or foreign occupation. This landai, composed during the Soviet occupation, continues to be recited today:

*May your airplane crash
and may the pilot die*

*that you are pouring
bombs on my
beloved Afghanistan.*

A 15-year-old girl named Lima wrote this four-line poem, called a *rubaiyat*, about the Taliban's restrictions on women:

*You won't allow me to go
to school.*

I won't become a doctor.

Remember this:

*One day you will be
sick.* [4]

AFGHAN CINEMA

Afghanistan had a small but well-regarded film industry during the 1960s and 1970s, before the Soviet occupation put an end to it. The Taliban also banned cinema, along with other forms of entertainment, and systematically destroyed much of the country's film archives. The industry has been revived in the twenty-first century, beginning with the 2003 release of the movie *Osama*, which is about a young girl who disguised herself as a boy in order to work during the Taliban era. Afghans living in other countries have also produced movies, including Afghan-American Jawed Wassel's *Firedancer* in 2004 and Afghan refugee Farid Faiz's *Ehsaas (Feelings)* in 2006.

The tradition of Afghans embracing poetry and literature is not new. When the Taliban was in power, women met secretly to discuss literature

Promotional posters for films being shown in Kabul, many of them Bollywood films from India, attract the attention of those passing by.

SPORTS

Buzkashi is a traditional sport in Afghanistan that is played on horseback. Two teams of riders try to gain and keep control of a headless goat carcass, called a *boz*. Traditionally the sport was played on the plains of northern Afghanistan. A more formalized version is now played in Kabul.

Afghans participate in some common modern sports as well, including cricket and soccer, which is called football in Afghanistan. The country participated in various sports in the Summer Olympics 12 times between 1936 and 2008, the year Afghanistan finally took home its first Olympic medal, for Tae Kwon Do. Two male Afghan Tae Kwon Do athletes competed in the Summer 2012 Olympic Games in London, England, and again took home a medal in the sport, tying for bronze with the United States. A female boxer from Kabul also competed in the 2012 Olympics. The first Afghan women athletes were allowed to participate in the Olympics in 2004.

under the guise of a sewing group called the Golden Needle. This is just one example of the way Afghan culture survives and thrives even in times of oppression, violence, or instability.

ARCHITECTURE

Many of Afghanistan's notable pieces of architecture were destroyed during the course of its history and have been replaced with more basic, modern construction. However, examples of historic building styles can still be found. Much of the country's Islamic architecture originated in the tenth and eleventh centuries, during the Ghaznavid and Ghorid Empires. The Minaret of Jam, one of Afghanistan's most famous landmarks, was constructed in 1194 by the Ghorid Empire, probably to commemorate the Ghorids' victory

The Minaret of Jam

The Shrine of Hazrat Ali, also known as the Blue
Mosque, in Mazar-e Sharif

over the Ghaznavids. The 213-foot (65 m) brick and tile spire stands
in a remote river valley in the province of Ghowr, west of Kabul. It has
been named a World Heritage Site by the United Nations Educational,
Scientific and Cultural Organization (UNESCO).

The Timurids favored bright and ornamental architecture with elaborately decorated citadels and large domes. One example of Timurid architecture is the Gawhar Shad mausoleum and madrassa complex in Herat. It was built in 1417 but has been mostly destroyed. In Balkh, the shrine of Khoja Abu Nasr Parsa, a mosque built in the 1460s, features a blue, ribbed dome and a large portal. Mazar-e Sharif, which means "noble shrine" in Dari, is the main city of the north. It takes its name from its large, blue-tiled shrine to Ali, the Prophet Muhammad's cousin and son-in-law.

Other notable mosques in Afghanistan include the No Gombad Mosque in Balkh, the oldest surviving mosque, which was built in 800–900 CE; the Friday Mosque in Herat, built in 1200 by the Ghorids; and the Shah Jahan Mosque in Kabul, constructed in 1647 by the same builder who created the Taj Mahal.

FOOD AND DRINK

Afghanistan's cuisine is somewhat similar to that of India or Iran, with lots of rice and bread. Afghan bread is called naan. In addition to being a staple, these flat sheets of seasoned bread are used as a serving dish for other foods and in place of utensils. Chunks of bread are torn off and used to pick up food and deliver it to the mouth. Rice is another common staple and is often served with meat, usually lamb or mutton, or vegetables. The national dish is *qabli pulao*, which is rice flavored with carrots, raisins, and almonds. Yogurt is another common food in Afghan cooking. It is dried in balls called *krut* so that it can be stored and later

> **Meals are usually served from a communal dish. Afghans always eat with their right hand.**

mixed with liquid to make sauces. Yogurt sauce is served with *mantu*, an Afghan ravioli stuffed with *ashak*, or meat, and leeks. Kebabs made with cubes of meat are also popular.

Street vendors in Afghanistan are called *tabang wallah*. A popular street snack is *boloni*, a fried pancake filled with potato, onions, greens, or squash. *Shor nakhod* is a piece of naan stuffed with stewed chickpeas and mint sauce. Tabang wallah also sell mantu and deep-fried fish, called *mahi*.

Tea, called chai in Afghanistan, is the national drink of choice. Afghans drink green or black tea sweetened with sugar or sucked through a sugar cube. *Chaikhana*, or teahouses, are found throughout urban areas. They typically serve pulao and kebabs along with a selection of tea. Chai plays an important role in Afghan society, particularly if offered by someone in his or her home, as it is a key part of hospitality. There are few gatherings in Afghanistan that do not feature chai, and discussion over chai is an important part of solving problems and making deals.

Mantu is usually stuffed with beef or lamb, which is steamed. It is often served during special occasions and gatherings.

CHAPTER 7

POLITICS: CONFLICT AND RESTORATION

At the end of 2001, most Afghans were rejoicing the fall of the Taliban regime and looking forward to enjoying more rights under a less oppressive government. That hope began dissipating within several years, however, as the national government struggled to maintain

THE AFGHAN FLAG

As different regimes took power, Afghanistan altered its national flag more times during the twentieth century than any other country in the world.[1] Another flag was adopted in 2002 after the fall of the Taliban. It features three vertical stripes of black, red, and green. The national emblem, which features a mosque, a pulpit, and flags on either side, is in the center. Below the mosque is the year of Afghan independence from Britain. An Arabic inscription says "God is great."

A soldier proudly hoists the national flag after graduating from Afghan military training. The nation strives to build a united, stable government as it rises from under Taliban control.

control of the country. Although the Taliban has been excluded from holding power in the government, it has persisted in the form of an insurgency. The Taliban insurgency grew, opposing the government through guerrilla war, including suicide bombings and IED attacks. Some rural areas of the country fell under the control of the Taliban or other local warlords and their militias. Even in areas of the country not controlled by the Taliban, the national government had difficulty enforcing its laws.

The next Afghan presidential election is slated for 2014, while US and NATO forces planned to leave by 2015, handing over control to the Afghan government and its own military. US Defense Secretary Leon Panetta felt confident that Afghanistan would be ready for the transition by then, pointing to the decreasing incidents of violence and the success of integrating some Taliban members into lawful society. "The Taliban has been weakened, Afghan army operations are progressing, and the reality is that the transition to Afghan security and governance is continuing and progressing," Panetta said in April 2012.[2]

Others wondered if the Taliban insurgency was merely waiting for the foreign security forces to leave before rising up again. As journalist Filkins said,

> "What Afghans are worried about is . . . as we [Americans] leave, the Afghan state, which we largely built, and the Afghan army, will not be able to hold the country together. . . . This is the fear, this is what people are worried about, this is what they're talking

Delegates lined up to vote on the new constitution in 2004.

about. . . . That basically the Taliban will come back some way, either by force, or they'll be brought into the government in a deal."[3]

Only time will tell whether Afghanistan's new government—plagued with allegations of corruption and struggling to offer effective governance throughout the country and unify the nation's disparate ethnic groups— will succeed.

NEW CONSTITUTION

After the fall of the Taliban in 2001, a group of officials from Afghanistan, neighboring countries, the United States, and the UN met in Bonn,

Germany, to establish an interim government for Afghanistan. The Bonn Agreement was signed on December 5, and Hamid Karzai was appointed as interim chairman. In June 2002, a loya jirga convened in Kabul with 1,450 delegates. The delegates represented all 362 administrative districts, with 160 seats set aside for women, 25 for nomadic groups, and 100 for refugees living in Iran and Pakistan. This assembly extended Karzai's leadership for two more years so a constitution could be written.

Next a 35-member constitutional commission, appointed by Karzai, convened. Its draft was presented to a new 500-member loya jirga in December 2003. This loya jirga approved the constitution on January 4, 2004. The constitution established the Republic of Afghanistan as an Islamic republic. Although it guarantees freedom of

LOYA JIRGA

The tradition of loya jirga is more than 1,000 years old in Afghanistan. When the country had a monarchy, a loya jirga made up of political, military, and religious leaders was convened to decide important matters such as selecting a new king, interpreting the constitution, or declaring war. Under the new constitution, a loya jirga can be called to amend the constitution, to prosecute charges against the president, or to consider other matters of national importance.

The loya jirga convened in a tent near the Intercontinental Hotel in Kabul.

religion, Islam is established as the official religion, and laws must abide by Islam.

The national government has three branches—executive, legislative, and judicial. The president, head of the executive branch, and two vice presidents are elected by popular vote. They can serve a maximum of two five-year terms. The president is both the chief of state and the head of the government. The executive branch also includes a cabinet of 25 ministers appointed by the president.

The legislative branch consists of a bicameral National Assembly. The upper house, known as the Meshrano Jirga, has 102 seats. One-third of its members are elected from provincial councils and serve four-year terms. Another third are elected from local district councils and serve three-year terms. The last third are nominated by the president

STRUCTURE OF THE GOVERNMENT OF AFGHANISTAN

Executive Branch	Legislative Branch	Judicial Branch
President Two Vice Presidents Cabinet	Meshrano Jirga Wolesi Jirga	Supreme Court

and serve five-year terms. The constitution requires that half of the appointed members be women. Members of the Wolesi Jirga, the lower house, are elected by popular vote. The Wolesi Jirga has no more than 250 members, who are elected to serve five-year terms. The judicial branch consists of a supreme court. Judges are appointed by the president and approved by the lower house. They can serve up to two four-year terms.

DEMOCRATIC ELECTIONS

Presidential elections took place for the first time ever under the new constitution on October 9, 2004. Security forces were prepared to keep the peace and prevent election tampering. Eight million Afghans, including refugees who were permitted to vote, cast their ballots, amounting to 75 percent of registered voters. Interim president Karzai was officially elected president with 55 percent of the vote.[4] Other candidates that year included Uzbek general Abdul Rashid Dostum, a former mujahideen commander; Shi'ite leader Muhammad Mohaqiq; Tajik leader Yunus Qanuni; and Masooda Jalal, the only female candidate.

More than 5,000 candidates ran in the first legislative election in September 2005. Turnout was lower in this election, with approximately half of the 12 million registered voters casting ballots.[5] Turnout was particularly low in Kabul, as well as in areas where the Taliban insurgency was strongest.

HAMID KARZAI

Hamid Karzai was born in 1957 in Kandahar, Afghanistan. Members of the Popalzai Pashtuns, the Karzai family fled to Pakistan during the Soviet occupation. In 1982, Karzai received his master's degree in political science from Himachal Pradesh University in India. He then returned to Afghanistan to join the mujahideen in overthrowing the Soviet government. From 1992 to 1994, he served as the deputy foreign minister for the coalition government formed by the mujahideen. He opposed the Taliban regime and moved back to Pakistan while they were in power. When the United States led a campaign to overthrow the Taliban, Karzai returned to offer his support.

By 2009, when the country was due to have its next presidential election, the security situation had worsened. The election was postponed from spring until August, when Karzai again won 55 percent of the vote.[6] However, due to voting irregularities, a runoff election was scheduled to take place on November 7, 2009, between Karzai and the second-place candidate, former foreign minister Abdullah Abdullah. However, Abdullah withdrew from the race days before the election, and Karzai took office for a second term.

President Karzai faces a great challenge in rebuilding Afghanistan.

Protesters in Lowgar accuse the governor of corruption in 2011 by waving a banner claiming he brought insecurity to the area.

INSTABILITY AND CHALLENGES

Afghanistan's government has struggled for legitimacy and effectiveness. While President Karzai started out with international support, many have criticized him for not doing enough to successfully develop and rebuild his country.

Corruption has also plagued the young government. Warlords and powerful regional commanders continued to have a great influence. Some officials were caught accepting bribes or using their positions for personal gain. Several politicians and officials have also been connected to the drug trade. In some cases, criminal leaders have even been selected for public office. Once in power, they have used their connections to appoint their criminal associates to positions in the government or to put militia fighters on the police force. Corruption has also been a problem for the police force. Anticorruption policies have been implemented to various degrees, but the corruption, along with many other government deficiencies, has caused many Afghans to become disillusioned about their government. In addition, Afghans face continuous economic hardships and security challenges. Nevertheless, a noticeable sense of improvement has developed in some urban areas such as Kabul, Mazar-e Sharif, and Herat.

CHAPTER 8

ECONOMICS: BUILDING INFRASTRUCTURE

Decades of conflict left Afghanistan's economy in tatters, as did several years of severe drought. From the 1950s to the 1970s, the country was able to expand its industry and infrastructure with help from foreign aid—mainly from the United States and the Soviet Union—as well as through natural gas sales to the Soviet Union. Much of this progress was undone during the civil war of the 1980s and 1990s. The economy sank even further under the Taliban regime. Most of the country's educated or skilled population left the country to avoid its harsh policies.

The economic situation has improved somewhat since the fall of the Taliban, bolstered in large part through foreign aid. Still, Afghanistan remains one of the poorest countries in the world. Many Afghans

Shoppers, traffic, and businesspeople in downtown Kabul in the spring of 2012

continue to lack adequate shelter, food, or medical care. There is also a lack of electric power. Afghanistan is also challenged because it is a landlocked country. Having no access to the sea limits its prospects for trade unless it partners with a neighboring country. Security issues have minimized opportunities for trade, industrial development, and employment, and violent conflicts have displaced families from their income sources.

For the year 2011, Afghanistan's gross domestic product (GDP) was an estimated $30.11 billion, ranking 110th out of 193 countries. The GDP was growing at an annual rate of 5.7 percent, the fifty-second-highest growth rate in the world. However, per capita GDP—the nation's total production divided by its population—was only $1,000, making it 213th on the list of the world's 226 ranked countries and territories. Unemployment is very high at an estimated 35 percent, but falling; in 2005, it was estimated at 40 percent. More than one-third of the population lives in poverty.[1]

AN AGRICULTURE-BASED ECONOMY

The Afghan economy is largely agriculture based, even though only 12 percent of the country's land is suitable for farming.[2] Many Afghans are subsistence farmers, meaning they grow food and raise livestock to

An Afghan man stands in front of his home in one of the many poor neighborhoods outside Kabul.

sustain their own family. Others are pastoral nomads, meaning they move from place to place in order to find pasture for their livestock.

Although solid statistics are hard to calculate for Afghanistan, it is estimated that more than 78 percent of the labor force works in agriculture, generating approximately 35 percent of the country's income. The country's main legal agricultural products are wheat, fruit, nuts, wool, mutton, sheepskin, and lambskin. A quarter of the gross national product (GNP) comes from industry. Some of the products produced include textiles such as handwoven carpets, soap, furniture, shoes, fertilizer, apparel, beverages, and cement. Approximately 40 percent of the GNP comes from services.[3]

EXPORTS AND IMPORTS

Afghanistan's main trade partners are Pakistan, India, the United States, Russia, Germany, and Tajikistan. In addition to a large illegal opium trade, the country's chief exports include fruit, nuts, handwoven carpets, wool, cotton, hides and pelts, and precious and semiprecious gems. Income from exports totaled $571 million in 2010. That same year, Afghanistan imported $5.3 billion worth of goods, including machinery, food, textiles, and petroleum products.[4]

Many of Afghanistan's economic difficulties have been caused by struggles in its agricultural sector. Some of the country's already-limited farmland, along with its fruit and nut orchards, was destroyed during several decades of war. A severe drought between 1998 and 2001 made the situation worse. Before the Soviet invasion, Afghanistan

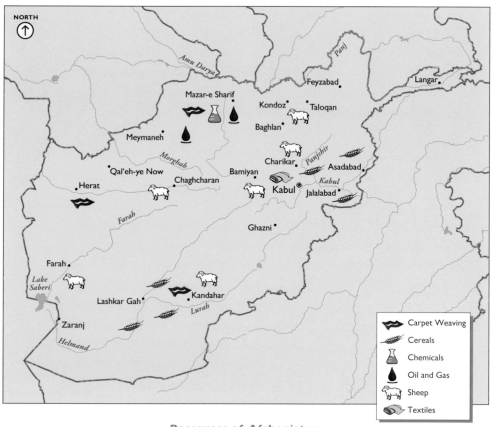

NORTH

Resources of Afghanistan

	Carpet Weaving
	Cereals
	Chemicals
	Oil and Gas
	Sheep
	Textiles

produced enough food to export more than it imported; as of 2009, that situation had reversed.

While most crops suffered in the post-Taliban area, one illicit crop thrived—opium poppies. Afghanistan is the world's largest producer of opium, a substance that is used to make the painkiller morphine as well as the illegal narcotic heroin. Opium poppies are grown primarily in the fertile northern plains. When the Taliban fell in 2001, opium production stood at approximately 185 short tons (168 metric tons) annually. By 2004, opium production had ballooned to 4,200 short tons (3,810 metric tons), amounting to 87 percent of the world's opium.[5] A blight affecting poppy plants brought production down to 3,200 short tons (2,903 metric tons) in 2010, still a significant amount.[6]

The opium drug trade has provided funding to local warlords, insurgent and criminal groups including the Taliban, and corrupt government officials who accept bribes. Additionally, the increase in opium cultivation means that fewer grains are grown to sustain the country's food supply. However, doing away with the opium industry would seriously damage many local economies in which farmers depend on these crops for income. More than 500,000 Afghan farm families made their living by growing opium as of 2009.[7] British and US efforts to curb opium production by destroying crops have been largely unsuccessful, resulting only in taking away the livelihood of some of these families. In 2009, Britain and the United States changed tactics, focusing on minimizing drug-trafficking criminal gangs rather than on curbing production.

An Afghan farmer harvests opium poppies from a field in Kandahar. The Afghan government often demolishes such fields in an effort to curb illegal growing and trading.

EFFORTS TO REBUILD

Afghanistan's economy has been bolstered by billions of dollars of foreign aid in recent years. Some of this aid funded repairs to portions of Afghanistan's war-damaged infrastructure. Highways and bridges were rebuilt to facilitate transportation and trade. Access to electricity has also improved since the fall of the Taliban.

Another goal of the United States and the international community is to reestablish rural lending services for Afghan farmers who need financing to purchase seeds and equipment. As of 2009, thousands of loans were extended to farmers and small businesses. These loans had a repayment rate of 94 percent.[8] Efforts to distribute seeds and fertilizer, remove dangerous explosive devices, and repair irrigation systems have also helped to restore the nation's agricultural potential.

CURRENCY

The Afghan currency is called the afghani. A new afghani was issued in 2002, with one new afghani worth the same as 1,000 old afghanis. The new afghani has been consistently valued at approximately 50 afghanis to one US dollar.[9]

Denominations of afghanis

Unlike some of its Middle Eastern neighbors, Afghanistan does not have a significant petroleum supply. However, it does have large natural gas reserves. Before the 1990s, Afghan natural gas was being piped to Uzbekistan and Tajikistan, but some natural gas deposits are still untapped. As of 2012, plans were taking shape for a natural gas pipeline across Afghanistan that would link Turkmenistan to Pakistan. If these plans go forward, such a pipeline could become a major source of income and employment for Afghans.

Geologic surveys have also discovered large amounts of minerals that could be mined, including iron, copper, uranium, lead, zinc, and chrome ore. Deposits of gold, silver, lithium, rock salt, barite, beryl, fluorspar, bauxite, tantalum, asbestos, mica, and sulfur have also been found. Security issues and infrastructure problems have made these resources difficult to access, but they could provide sources of income for the country in the future.

Internet access is improving in Kabul due to many new Internet cafés.

Bolstering the tourism industry is another hope for future income. Afghanistan enjoyed a flourishing tourism industry during the 1970s, when approximately 120,000 people visited each year, helping support local economies. However, decades of violence and unrest changed that. As of 2012, the Afghanistan Tourism Organization estimated the country sees between 3,000 and 4,000 tourists annually.[10] Afghans hope that as stability increases, tourists will once again want to experience their country's heritage and rugged scenery, helping to boost their struggling economy. As Ghulam Nabi Farahi, the country's deputy minister for tourism, stated, "If there is security, people will come because of the hospitality, the good food, and the music."[11]

Afghanistan has approximately 50 airports.

CHAPTER 9
AFGHANISTAN TODAY

Afghan society is built around the traditions of family, religion, and community. Extended families often live together, and children do not leave home until they marry and start their own families. Travel writer Paul Clammer explained how the Afghan emphasis on family has evolved out of hardship and tribal practices:

> *Afghans are a naturally conservative people, and deeply religious. Their independence comes from the harshness of the country, where arable land is at a premium and the difficulties of the terrain has promoted self-reliance and inhibited the formation of strong central governments. As a result power has devolved down to the tribe,*

Family is important to Afghans, and many live with or spend much time with their extended family members.

village, and—central to Afghan life—the family. The household and mosque are the cornerstones of the community.[1]

In rural areas, extended families either live in one shared house or in a compound with several houses. The simple mud-brick shacks common in Afghanistan typically lack plumbing or electricity. Urban families have more modern homes or apartments, though only the very wealthy have all of the modern amenities. These dwellings are often furnished with mats or cushions.

For Afghan children, much of the day consists of schoolwork and chores. As Muslims, they also pray five times each day in keeping with their religion's guidelines. When they have free time, Afghan children enjoy playing games, dancing, or listening to music. In cities, some families even have a television and are able to watch American cartoons. For boys, kite flying is a favorite activity,

KITE FLYING

Kite flying, except when banned by the Taliban, has long been a popular pastime for Afghan boys. Simple kites are constructed out of scraps of paper or plastic mounted on a wire frame. *Gudiparan bazi*, or kite fighting, is also popular. Players attach bits of glass to their kite's string with glue. They then try to rub their string against their opponent's while flying in order to snap the string with the glass. Then the players race to find the fallen kite.

Flying kites is a popular social activity for Afghan boys of all ages.

although it is considered socially unacceptable for girls to participate in outdoor sports.

Relationships between boys and girls in Afghanistan are very different from those in Western countries such as the United States. Girls are very restricted in what they can do outside the home, particularly outside of cosmopolitan Kabul. Even in areas where girls attend school, they do so separately from boys. In fact, most social activities are segregated, and almost all marriages are arranged between the families of the bride and groom.

ARRANGED MARRIAGES

Most marriages in Afghanistan are still arranged. The bride's family, usually represented by her mother or aunts, negotiates with the groom's family over the details. The bride usually has a dowry consisting of jewelry, textiles, and household goods. The groom's family must pay a sum of money to the bride's family, called a *mahr*, or "bride price." Sometimes a family living in poverty will agree to an unfavorable marriage because it needs the money it will make from the mahr.

EDUCATION

Afghanistan's education system is slowly being rebuilt after decades of deterioration. During the Soviet occupation, many teachers and students,

Afghan teenagers study at a girls' school in Lashkar Gah.

facing torture or imprisonment, left the country. Other Afghans were deprived of education while living in refugee camps. Under the Taliban, girls were not allowed to attend school. After the Taliban fell, the country still lacked facilities for education, as well as educated adults qualified to be teachers. Taliban insurgents have continued to target schools, destroying more than 400 schools in the south in 2007 and 2008.[2] But as of 2012, 8 million Afghan children were enrolled in school, approximately 40 percent of whom were girls.[3] However, in 2012, 6 million Afghan children still did not have access to education.[4]

Grade school is free to attend, and attendance is legally required in areas where it is available. Most Afghan schools are much more primitive than schools in more developed countries. In many communities, classes take place in a tent, with students sitting on the ground. If a school isn't large enough to hold all of its students, different

AFGHAN MEDIA

Recent improvements in freedom of speech have allowed Afghanistan's media industry to take off. More than 300 newspapers and magazines are now being published.[5] Most of these publications are aligned with a political group, with few strides being made toward independent journalism. Radio is another source of news, as well as entertainment. A national radio station has been broadcasting since the 1920s, but new stations have started to provide competition. Where electricity is available, Afghans also enjoy television shows, both those made by Afghans and those from other countries in the region, particularly India. Popular shows include news programs and music videos.

age groups meet in the morning and afternoon. In addition to reading and writing, students learn subjects including religion, science, math, and history.

Some adult-education programs have also been implemented to compensate for the lack of formal education in past decades. Approximately 28 percent of the Afghan population is literate, including 43.1 percent of men and 12.6 percent of women.[6]

WOMEN'S RIGHTS

After years of suffering under the oppressive Taliban regime, women have started making slow strides forward in Afghanistan. Officially, women were awarded the rights to vote, attend school, seek employment, and even hold public office by the 2004 constitution. Women were included in the assembly that approved the constitution and are

CLOTHING: BURQAS AND DRESS CODES

In the post-Taliban era, Afghans no longer have to follow strict dress codes that require men to wear beards and women to cover every inch of their skin. However, Afghan dress continues to be largely conservative due to Islamic tradition. Women commonly wear a burqa, a billowing garment that covers the entire body. Even those who do not wear a burqa typically wear a hijab, a scarf that covers the hair. Men usually wear baggy trousers and a long shirt with sleeves.

guaranteed a certain number of seats in the legislature. Female candidates for higher office—such as Masooda Jalal, who ran for president in 2004—have brought further attention to issues affecting Afghan women. Jalal served as minister of women's affairs in Karzai's administration along with two other women.

> **More than two-thirds of Afghans do not have access to safe drinking water.**

However, Afghan women are still struggling to be treated as equals, especially in rural areas. Many women in these areas are still kept in seclusion and prevented from attending school or working outside the home. Illiteracy, inadequate health care, and violence against women continue to be problems. Women's rights activists have been repeatedly threatened with violence. Safia Amajan, head of the provincial women's affairs department in Kandahar, was assassinated in 2006. Malalai Joya, an outspoken legislator, has received death threats. Female students and teachers who educate girls have also been threatened. Despite these obstacles, Afghans seem committed to furthering women's rights. One survey in 2010 found that 87 percent of men and women interviewed supported a woman's right to attend school, and 64 percent responded that women should be allowed to work outside the home.[7]

CHALLENGES AND HOPE

More than a decade after the end of Taliban rule, Afghanistan has seen much progress. Afghans no longer live under the oppressive rule of a regime that abused human rights and supported terrorism. They are enjoying more rights and making progress in areas such as education and health care.

But many challenges still remain for Afghans. Wars have scarred the land and destroyed valuable infrastructure, leaving Afghanistan as one of the poorest countries in the world and dependent on foreign aid. A weak central government has been unable to squash the Taliban insurgency, particularly in the south, while warlords and violent criminals go largely unchecked. The illegal opium trade provides a livelihood for many of the nation's farmers, yet it is also the root of much government corruption.

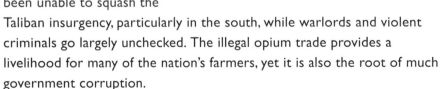

HEALTH CARE

While Afghanistan still has one of the highest mortality rates in the world, the health care situation is improving. In 2002, only 9 percent of the population had access to health care within a one-hour traveling distance. By 2012, that number had increased to 85 percent, though much of that health care is not very advanced.[8]

With foreign troops scheduled to leave in 2015, some wonder whether the Afghan army will be able to maintain order and continue to fight off the Taliban on its own. According to journalist Filkins, this is what a peaceful future for Afghanistan hinges on: "The fix is the Afghan army. . . . If it's good enough . . . the state holds together. If it's not good enough, then it falls apart. . . . The question is can it stand on its own?

Fifty countries had contributed troops to the International Security Assistance Force in Afghanistan in 2012.

Can it fight the Taliban on its own?"[9] But Afghans have long been known for their fierce independence and survival skills. Many look forward to being free of foreign interference in their culture and depending on their own people to fulfill their hopes for a better tomorrow.

As a nation, the Afghans share a collective independent spirit that will help them rise to the challenge of rebuilding their nation.

TIMELINE

ca. 2000 BCE	Aryan tribes arrive in the area now known as Afghanistan and found the city of Balkh.
ca. 550 BCE	Cyrus II leads the Persians into Afghanistan.
331 BCE	Alexander the Great expands his Macedonian Empire into Afghanistan.
135 BCE	A group of tribes known as the Kushans begin four centuries of rule over Afghanistan.
652 CE	The Arabs invade Afghanistan, beginning 500 years of Islamic rule.
1219	Mongolian ruler Genghis Khan leads 200,000 Mongol warriors into Afghanistan.
1504	Babur, a descendent of Genghis Khan, captures Kabul. He soon founds the Mughal Empire.
1747	Persian ruler Nadir Shah is assassinated. Ahmad Shah Durrani, known as the father of modern Afghanistan, takes power.
1839	Great Britain invades Afghanistan, beginning the First Anglo-Afghan War.
1878	The Second Anglo-Afghan War begins.
1879	Ya'qub Khan signs the Treaty of Gandamak, giving Britain authority over Afghanistan. This triggers a civil war.
1881	'Abd al-Rahman Khan, considered by some to be the founder of modern Afghanistan, takes power.

1919	King Amanullah leads an attack against British-controlled India in May, triggering the Third Anglo-Afghan War.
1919	The Treaty of Rawalpindi establishes Afghanistan's independence from Britain on August 8.
1923	King Amanullah proclaims the country's first constitution.
1933	Zahir Shah, the last king of Afghanistan, comes to power after the assassination of Mohammad Nader Shah.
1964	A loya jirga approves a new constitution that establishes a constitutional monarchy with a bicameral legislature.
1973	Mohammad Daud Khan seizes power in a bloodless coup and ends the monarchy.
1979	The Soviet Union invades Afghanistan in December, beginning nine years of Soviet occupation and civil war.
1996	The Taliban completes its rise to power and establishes the Islamic Emirate of Afghanistan.
2001	Coalition forces led by the United States overthrow the Taliban and install an interim government.
2004	A new constitution is adopted on January 4.
2004	Hamid Karzai is elected president on October 9 in Afghanistan's first democratic election.
2009	Karzai is reelected for another presidential term.

FACTS AT YOUR FINGERTIPS

GEOGRAPHY

Official name: Islamic Republic of Afghanistan (in Dari, Jomhuri-ye Eslami-ye Afghanestan)

Area: 251,827 square miles (652,230 sq km)

Climate: Arid to semiarid, with cold winters and hot summers

Highest elevation: Mount Nowshak, 24,557 feet (7,485 m) above sea level

Lowest elevation: Amu Darya, 846 feet (258 m) above sea level

Significant geographic features: Hindu Kush Mountains, Amu Darya River

PEOPLE

Population (July 2012 est.): 30,419,928

Most populous city: Kabul

Ethnic groups: Pashtun, 42 percent; Tajik, 27 percent; Hazara, 9 percent; Uzbek, 9 percent; Aimak, 4 percent; Turkmen, 3 percent; Baloch, 2 percent; other, 4 percent

Percentage of residents living in urban areas: 23 percent

Life expectancy: 49.72 years at birth (world rank: 217)

Language(s): Dari (official), 50 percent; Pashto (official), 35 percent; Turkic languages (primarily Uzbek and Turkmen), 11 percent; 30 minor languages (primarily Balochi and Pashai), 4 percent

Religion(s): Sunni Muslim, 80 percent; Shia Muslim, 19 percent; other, 1 percent

GOVERNMENT AND ECONOMY

Government: Islamic republic

Capital: Kabul

Date of adoption of current constitution: January 4, 2004

Head of state: president

Head of government: president

Legislature: National assembly consisting of Meshrano Jirga and Wolesi Jirga

Currency: afghani

Industries and natural resources: agriculture; small-scale production of textiles, soap, furniture, shoes, fertilizer, apparel, food products, nonalcoholic beverages, mineral water, and cement; handwoven carpets; natural gas, coal, copper

NATIONAL SYMBOLS

Holidays: Independence Day is celebrated on August 19, commemorating independence from Britain in 1919. Nawruz, or New Year's Day, is celebrated on the first day of spring. Muslim holidays are also recognized.

Flag: Three vertical bands of black, red, and green, with the national emblem in white in the center

National anthem: "Milli Surood"

National animal: None, but the lion is considered a national symbol

KEY PEOPLE

Genghis Khan, Mongolian ruler who invaded in 1219

Ahmad Shah Durrani, founded the Durrani Empire in 1747 and is considered the father of modern Afghanistan

Hamid Karzai, first president of the Islamic Republic of Afghanistan

PROVINCES OF AFGHANISTAN

Province; Capital

Badakhshan; Feyzabad

Badghis; Qal'eh-ye Now

Baghlan; Pol-e Khomri

Balkh; Mazar-e Sharif

Bamiyan; Bamiyan

Daykondi; Nili

Farah; Farah

Faryab; Meymaneh

Ghazni; Ghazni

Ghowr; Chaghcharan

Helmand; Lashkar Gah

Herat; Herat

Jowzjan; Sheberghan

Kabul; Kabul

Kandahar; Kandahar

Kapisa; Mahmud-e Raqi

Khowst; Khowst

Konar; Asadabad

Kondoz; Kondoz

Laghman; Mehtar Lam

Lowgar; Pol-e 'Alam

Nangarhar; Jalalabad

Nimruz; Zaranj

Nurestan; Parun

Oruzgan; Tarin Kowt

Paktia; Gardiz

Paktika; Sharan

Panjshir; Bazarak

Parwan; Charikar

Samangan; Samangan

Sar-e Pol; Sar-e Pol

Takhar; Taloqan

Vardak; Meydan Shahr

Zabol; Qalat

GLOSSARY

Buddhism

A religion based on the teachings of Gautama Buddha, an Indian prince from the sixth century BCE who renounced court life in order to seek enlightenment.

communism

An economic system defined by collective ownership of property and the organization of labor for the common advantage; a government system in which a single party holds power and the state controls the economy.

deciduous

A type of plant or tree that sheds its leaves annually.

dynasty

A succession of rulers from the same family or line.

fast

To refrain from eating.

ideology

Beliefs and principles for which a person or a political party stands.

insurgency

A revolt against civil authority or an established government; an organized group of people engaged in such a revolt.

monsoon

A large-scale wind system that seasonally blows in opposite directions and affects the climate of a region.

Mughal

A leader descended from a conquering Islamic tribe; also *Mogul*.

nomadic

The seasonally traveling lifestyle of a group of people who have no fixed residence.

refugee

A person who flees to a foreign country to escape danger or persecution.

regime

A mode of rule or management.

secular

Nonreligious.

shah

Ruler.

socialism

An economic system in which the government controls the means of production and distribution of goods.

ADDITIONAL RESOURCES

SELECTED BIBLIOGRAPHY

Clammer, Paul. *Afghanistan*. Melbourne, Austral.: Lonely Planet, 2007. Print.

Omrani, Bijan, and Matthew Leeming. *Afghanistan: A Companion and Guide*. Hong Kong: Odyssey, 2011. Print.

Runion, Meredith. *The History of Afghanistan*. Westport, CT: Greenwood, 2007. Print.

Wahab, Shaista, and Barry Youngerman. *A Brief History of Afghanistan*. New York: Facts on File, 2007. Print.

FURTHER READINGS

Berlatsky, Noah. *Afghanistan*. San Diego: Greenhaven, 2010. Print.

Ellis, Deborah. *Kids of Kabul: Living Bravely Through a Never-Ending War*. Toronto: Groundwood, 2012. Print.

Steele, Philip. *Afghanistan: From War to Peace?* London: Wayland, 2011. Print.

WEB LINKS

To learn more about Afghanistan, visit ABDO Publishing Company online at **www.abdopublishing.com**. Web sites about Afghanistan are featured on our Book Links page. These links are routinely monitored and updated to provide the most current information available.

PLACES TO VISIT

If you are ever in Afghanistan, consider checking out these important and interesting sites!

Buddhas of Bamiyan

The Kushans carved the world's largest Buddha statues into a cliff in the Bamiyan Mountains northwest of Kabul. The two statues were destroyed by the Taliban in 2001, but their remnants are still a popular destination for tourists.

Gardens of Babur

Restored after the fall of the Taliban, the gardens in central Kabul surround the tomb of Mughal ruler Babur, designed by the same architect as India's Taj Mahal.

Kabul Museum

Much of the Kabul Museum's collection was destroyed in times of war or by the Taliban, but the museum recently reopened with an impressive display of salvaged and restored artwork.

SOURCE NOTES

CHAPTER 1. A VISIT TO AFGHANISTAN

1. "*The Forever War* by Dexter Filkins: Author Q & A." *Powell's City of Books*. Powells.com, n.d. Web. 9 Oct. 2012.

2. Joshua Hammer. "The Mysteries of Kabul." *New York Times*. New York Times, 21 Jan. 2007. Web. 9 Oct. 2012.

3. Ibid.

4. "Afghanistan War." *Encyclopædia Britannica*. Encyclopædia Britannica, 2012. Web. 9 Oct. 2012.

5. "Ask the Author Live: Dexter Filkins on Afghanistan." *The New Yorker*. Condé Nast, 27 June 2011. Web. 9 Oct. 2012.

CHAPTER 2. GEOGRAPHY: MOUNTAINS AND DESERT

1. Shaista Wahab and Barry Youngerman. *A Brief History of Afghanistan*. New York: Facts on File, 2007. Print. 5.

2. Bijan Omrani and Matthew Leeming. *Afghanistan: A Companion and Guide*. Hong Kong: Odyssey, 2011. Print. 231.

3. Afghanistan." *Encyclopædia Britannica*. Encyclopædia Britannica, 2012. Web. 9 Oct. 2012.

4. "Afghanistan." *BBC: Weather*. BBC, n.d. Web. 9 Oct. 2012.

5. "Afghanistan." *Encyclopædia Britannica*. Encyclopædia Britannica, 2012. Web. 9 Oct. 2012.

6. "Afghanistan." *Weatherbase*. Canty and Associates, n.d. Web. 16 Aug. 2012.

CHAPTER 3. ANIMALS AND NATURE: RETURNING DIVERSITY

1. "*Panthera uncial*." *IUCN Red List of Threatened Species*. International Union for Conservation of Nature and Natural Resources, 2011. Web. 9 Oct. 2012.

2. Paul Clammer. *Afghanistan*. Melbourne, Austral.: Lonely Planet, 2007. Print. 65.

3. "UNEP in Afghanistan." *United Nations Environment Programme*. United Nations Environment Programme, Jan. 2009. Web. 9 Oct. 2012.

4. "Summary Statistics: Summaries by Country, Table 5, Threatened Species in Each Country." *IUCN Red List of Threatened Species*. International Union for Conservation of Nature and Natural Resources, 2010. Web. 9 Oct. 2012.

5. "UNEP in Afghanistan." *United Nations Environment Programme*. United Nations Environment Programme, Jan. 2009. Web. 9 Oct. 2012.

6. "Animals in Afghanistan Survive Conflict (video)." *TIME Video*. Time, 2012. Web. 9 Oct. 2012.

7. "UNEP in Afghanistan." *United Nations Environment Programme*. United Nations Environment Programme, Jan. 2009. Web. 9 Oct. 2012.

8. Abdullah Qazi. "Biography: Mustafa Zahir." *Afghanistan Online*. n.p, 28 May 2010. Web. 9 Oct. 2012.

9. "Afghanistan's First National Park." *Wildlife Conservation Society*. Wildlife Conservation Society, 2012. Web. 9 Oct. 2012.

10. Jason Strasiuso. "Band-e-Amir Declared as Afghanistan's First National Park." *HuffPost World*. Huffingtonpost.com, 18 June 2009. Web. 9 Oct. 2012.

11. Ibid.

CHAPTER 4. HISTORY: INVASIONS, UNREST, AND REVIVAL

1. Thomas Barfield. *Afghanistan: A Cultural and Political History*. Princeton, NJ: Princeton UP, 2010. Print. 81.

2. Meredith Runion. *The History of Afghanistan*. Westport, CT: Greenwood Press, 2007. 81.

3. Ibid. 111–113.

4. Ibid. 114–115.

CHAPTER 5. PEOPLE: DIVERSITY AND INDEPENDENCE

1. "The World Factbook: Afghanistan." *Central Intelligence Agency*. Central Intelligence Agency, 5 Oct. 2012. Web. 9 Oct. 2012.

2. Ibid.

3. Ibid.

4. Shaista Wahab and Barry Youngerman. *A Brief History of Afghanistan*. New York: Facts on File, 2007. Print. 18.

5. Thomas Barfield. *Afghanistan: A Cultural and Political History*. Princeton, NJ: Princeton UP, 2010. Print. 55–56.

6. "The World Factbook: Afghanistan." *Central Intelligence Agency*. Central Intelligence Agency, 5 Oct. 2012. Web. 9 Oct. 2012.

7. "Pashtun." *Encyclopædia Britannica*. Encyclopædia Britannica, 2012. Web. 9 Oct. 2012.

8. Thomas Barfield. *Afghanistan: A Cultural and Political History*. Princeton, NJ: Princeton UP, 2010. Print. 44.

9. Shaista Wahab and Barry Youngerman. *A Brief History of Afghanistan*. New York: Facts on File, 2007. Print. 39.

10. "The World Factbook: Afghanistan." *Central Intelligence Agency*. Central Intelligence Agency, 5 Oct. 2012. Web. 9 Oct. 2012.

11. Ibid.

12. Shaista Wahab and Barry Youngerman. *A Brief History of Afghanistan*. New York: Facts on File, 2007. Print. 259.

13. "Insecurity Lowers Afghan Returns 2009, UN Reports." *UN News Centre*. UN News Centre, 29 Dec. 2009. Web. 9 Oct. 2012.

SOURCE NOTES CONTINUED

14. "The World Factbook: Afghanistan." *Central Intelligence Agency*. Central Intelligence Agency, 5 Oct. 2012. Web. 9 Oct. 2012.

15. "Country Comparison: Life Expectancy at Birth." *Central Intelligence Agency*. Central Intelligence Agency, 5 Oct. 2012. Web. 9 Oct. 2012.

CHAPTER 6. CULTURE: THRIVING TRADITIONS

1. Mark T. McCord. "An Analysis of Business Opportunities within Afghanistan's Carpet Sector." *International Trade Administration*. US Department of Commerce, May 2007. Web. 10 Oct. 2012.

2. "The World Factbook: Afghanistan." *Central Intelligence Agency*. Central Intelligence Agency, 5 Oct. 2012. Web. 9 Oct. 2012.

3. Eliza Griswold. "Why Afghan Women Risk Death to Write Poetry." *New York Times*. New York Times, 27 Apr. 2012. Web. 10 Oct. 2012.

4. Ibid.

CHAPTER 7. POLITICS: CONFLICT AND RESTORATION

1. "The World Factbook: Afghanistan." *Central Intelligence Agency*. Central Intelligence Agency, 5 Oct. 2012. Web. 9 Oct. 2012.

2. "Media Availability with Secretaries Clinton and Panetta at the NATO Ministerial." *US Department of Defense: News Transcript*. US Department of Defense, 18 Apr. 2012. Web. 10 Oct. 2012.

3. "Dexter Filkins of the *New Yorker* on Afghanistan (video)." *Charlie Rose*. Charlie Rose, 10 July 20102. Web. 10 Oct. 2012.

4. Shaista Wahab and Barry Youngerman. *A Brief History of Afghanistan*. New York: Facts on File, 2007. Print. 240.

5. Ibid. 241.

6. "Afghan Election Results Give Karzai 55% of Vote." *CBC News: World*. CBC, 16 Sep. 2009. Web. 10 Oct. 2012.

CHAPTER 8. ECONOMICS: BUILDING INFRASTRUCTURE

1. "The World Factbook: Afghanistan." *Central Intelligence Agency*. Central Intelligence Agency, 5 Oct. 2012. Web. 9 Oct. 2012.

2. Shaista Wahab and Barry Youngerman. *A Brief History of Afghanistan*. New York: Facts on File, 2007. Print. 7.

3. "The World Factbook: Afghanistan." *Central Intelligence Agency*. Central Intelligence Agency, 5 Oct. 2012. Web. 9 Oct. 2012.

4. Ibid.

5. Shaista Wahab and Barry Youngerman. *A Brief History of Afghanistan*. New York: Facts on File, 2007. Print. 249.

6. "Field Listing: Illegal Drugs." *Central Intelligence Agency*. Central Intelligence Agency, n.d. Web. 10 Oct. 2012.

7. "Can Anyone Pacify An Opium State?" *CBS News*. CBS Interactive, 1 Apr. 2012. Web. 10 Oct. 2012.

8. "U.S. Relations With Afghanistan." *US Department of State*. US Department of State, 6 Sep. 2012. Web. 10 Oct. 2012.

9. Paul Clammer. *Afghanistan*. Melbourne, Austral.: Lonely Planet, 2007. Print. 206.

10. Lianne Gutcher. "Ongoing Conflict Severely Limits Tourism in Afghanistan." *USA Today: News*. USA Today/Gannet Co., 27 May 2012. Web. 10 Oct. 2012.

11. Ibid.

CHAPTER 9. AFGHANISTAN TODAY

1. Paul Clammer. *Afghanistan*. Melbourne, Austral.: Lonely Planet, 2007. Print. 41.

2. Shaheen Buneri. "Pakistan's Swat Valley: Taliban Gone But Peace Remains Elusive." *Pulitzer Center on Crisis Reporting*. Pulitzer Center on Crisis Reporting, 10 Jan. 2012. Web. 10 Oct. 2012.

3. "How US Aid Lifts Afghans." *Christian Science Monitor*. Christian Science Monitor, 21 July 2012. Web. 10 Oct. 2012.

4. "6 Million Afghan Children are Deprived of Education." *Ariana News*. Ariana News, n.d. Web. 10 Oct. 2012.

5. Paul Clammer. *Afghanistan*. Melbourne, Austral.: Lonely Planet, 2007. Print. 57–58.

6. "The World Factbook: Afghanistan." *Central Intelligence Agency*. Central Intelligence Agency, 5 Oct. 2012. Web. 9 Oct. 2012.

7. Ruth Rene, ed. "Afghanistan in 2010: A Survey of the Afghan People." *Asia Foundation*. Asia Foundation, 2010. Web. 10 Oct. 2012.

8. "101/2012: Armed Forces Answer British Museum's Call to Return Stolen Artefacts to Kabul." *Ministry of Defence*. Gov.uk, 19 July 2012. Web. 10 Oct. 2012.

9. "Dexter Filkins of the *New Yorker* on Afghanistan (video)." *Charlie Rose*. Charlie Rose, 10 July 20102. Web. 10 Oct. 2012.

INDEX

PHOTO CREDITS